# Praise for *Night*

'An inspiring and uplifting book about finding infinite value in the most intense and painful experience of profound loss'
**Sandie Shaw**

'This beautifully written memoir charts Diane's personal anguish as her son Sacha – once a powerful and vibrant young man – is lost to the full-on white-knuckle ride of heroin addiction. In essence it is a book about finding value in profound loss'
**Marina Cantacuzino, author of *Forgiveness***

'A heart-wrenching and uplifting story of one woman's tragedy, transformation and, ultimately, triumph, made all the more powerful because every word is true – and because Diane Esguerra is a very fine writer'
**Edward Canfor-Dumas**

'Takes you on a geographical and spiritual journey to a place of healing and ultimately to a place of peace in mind and heart. For anyone going through the grief journey of losing a loved one to addiction, I highly recommend this mother's story. Ultimately, you will feel uplifted and strengthened by sharing this journey with her'
**Elizabeth Burton-Phillips, author of *Mum, Can You Lend Me Twenty Quid?***

'Diane Esguerra's eloquent writing and self-deprecating humour make this a surprisingly rewarding and uplifting read. The journey is a courageous one; so too is her willingness to share raw emotion with her reader and her determination to create both meaning and value out of some truly heart-breaking life experiences'
**Therapy Today**

DIANE ESGUERRA is a writer and a psychotherapist. She studied English at University College, London, followed by a stint at drama school, and later trained as a psychotherapist at the University of Sussex. For a number of years she worked as a performance artist in Britain, Europe and the United States.

Diane has written for both theatre and television and is the recipient of a Geneva-Europe Television Award and a *Time Out* Theatre Award. Her books include *The Oshun Diaries* (Eye Books, 2019) and *Buddhism and Loss* (Mud Pie Books, 2023). A previous version of the present book was published as *Junkie Buddha* by Eye Books in 2015.

The founder and director of Greenlight Counselling Consultancy, she lives in Dorset with her husband David and dog Chico.

www.dianeesguerra.com

1

# night into light

a mother's journey of grief
and transformation

**diane esguerra**

Ⓞ

Published in 2024
by Eye Books Ltd
29A Barrow Street
Much Wenlock
Shropshire
TF13 6EN

www.eye-books.com

ISBN: 9781785633911

Cover design by Nell Wood
Typeset in Horley Old Style and Brandon Grotesque

British Library Cataloguing in Publication Data
A catalogue record for this book is available from the British Library.

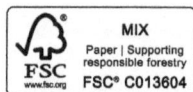

MIX
Paper | Supporting
responsible forestry
FSC
www.fsc.org   FSC® C013604

For Sacha

# contents

# foreword

Have you ever had to face your worst fear? If the answer is 'yes', I assume you survived the experience or you wouldn't be reading this. Was it traumatic? Did it change you? In 2005 I faced my worst fear – or rather my worst fear ambushed me; I had no choice in the matter. My son Sacha, my only child, died. And yes, it was traumatic and it also changed me.

'Trauma' has become an overused label to describe the fall-out from a plethora of unwanted events in our lives – from losing a smartphone to being in a serious car crash. I can assure you that the trauma I experienced followed the *Cambridge Dictionary* definition: 'severe and lasting emotional shock and pain caused by an extremely upsetting experience'.

At the time I had to face my worst fear I was (and still am) a psychotherapist, but any coping tools I may have acquired up to that point in my training – and, for that matter, in my life – were useless in the face of the ferocious onslaught of this genuinely traumatic event.

What I have come to understand, however, is that worst fears, when realised, can also open up entirely new vistas – if you feel brave enough to look around you. Sure, some of those landscapes are bleak, suffused with pain and despair, but others can prove transformational, illuminating parts of yourself that you never knew existed.

I decided to go on a healing journey. At first this took the shape of a physical journey to another land, but my journey didn't end there. It segued into a quest to discover how to survive and thrive in my new reality. This journey has given me a deeper understanding of what it means to be truly human. I'm still on it and probably will be for the remainder of my life.

Diane Esguerra
2024

# lost treasures of the world

## why me?

I never thought it would happen to me. It happened to other mothers – yes, and fathers too. I'd seen them on the evening news, puffy-eyed, bewildered, blinking away tears. The camera zooms in to the photograph of the son as they like to remember him, in his school blazer (eyes still shining then) grinning toothlessly at the school photographer. Or the daughter as a teenager, astride a mountain bike in the Pyrenees, tanned and ponytailed.

I never thought it would happen to me. But in 2005 it did. I discovered my child Sacha, a man now, a man who had never practised yoga, slumped over in child-pose on a beer-stained rug; his alabaster back cold to my touch; a half-empty syringe at his side; daytime television drowned out by the weeping of his dogs and the howling of police sirens.

My future ambushed.

These mothers on television – clutching handkerchiefs or their husbands' hands – I used to think they put themselves through this ordeal in order to draw the public's attention to a pressing social issue, start a campaign, establish a foundation to honour his or her memory. But then I understood they do it to avoid waking up in the morning with the feeling that the very heart of their lives has been surgically extracted without anaesthetic. Although they yearn to escape to the realm into which the beloved has made an untimely entry – without their permission – they're too considerate to inflict this same agony on their living loved ones. So what do they do instead? They search for meaning; for a purpose to rein themselves back from the lurking abyss.

In the weeks that followed Sacha's death I duly busied myself applying to a charitable trust for funding to set up a project to help teenagers who had been abused in childhood and who would, more than likely, go on to self-harm, harm others or abuse substances. But my burnt-out heart wasn't really in it. I needed a break from that all-too-familiar world, and it was a relief when the funding didn't come through.

The void continued to terrorise me. As a Buddhist I believed in the preciousness of life and the concept of 'turning poison into medicine': that suffering – however deep – could ultimately prove beneficial. But what value could possibly be created from this?

My daily mantra had become 'Why me?… Why me?'

'I'm not a junkie, Mum,' Sacha used to say. 'I'm someone with a habit.'

And I'd convinced myself I could help him break that habit. Defeat wasn't an option I'd allowed myself to consider; too much was at stake.

My son wasn't the archetypal junkie you see in the movies with hollowed-out, shifty eyes, greasy hair and thieving, nicotine-stained fingers. Yes, he smoked roll-ups, but that was as far as it went. More than he loved heroin, Sacha loved ancient Hispanic history and climbing mountains.

For Christmas, the week before his death, he'd given me a large, glossy, illustrated book called *Lost Treasures of the World*. I read how the Conquistador Francisco Pizarro captured the Inca emperor Atahualpa in Peru and promised him his freedom if his people were able to fill a 'ransom room' full of gold. For months the Incas laboured day and night to bring gold and treasure from all over their empire. But once the ransom room was full, Pizarro killed Atahualpa anyway.

How I empathised with those Incas who, like me, had done everything, everything in their power, to save the person in danger. How cheated they must have felt after his death.

How cheated I felt.

It was, he said, the best Christmas he'd had for years. We had tears in our eyes as Sacha played the blues again on his harmonica. Finally on a decent drugs programme, he'd turned a corner at last, I thought. Then, after some crazy partying on New Year's Eve, one last fling resulted in what the coroner recorded as 'accidental death from a heroin overdose'.

And I lost my treasure.

Peru stayed with me, though. Sacha's ashes sat in a wooden urn – not on the mantelpiece but, out of respect for his shyness, tucked away in a corner of the living room under the voluminous palm tree he'd bought me many Mother's Days ago. The ashes wanted to be scattered – but where? I already knew. I'd known all along.

For the last few years of his life, all Sacha had wanted was to go back to South America. Brought up in England but half Colombian, he'd travelled the continent extensively and had hiked the Inca Trail before it became a popular gap-year thing. He often recalled the moment when, dead on his feet with hunger and exhaustion, he reached the end of the trail and felt his spirit soar as he watched the sun rise over the Inca citadel of Machu Picchu.

'One of the coolest moments of my life, Mum. When I'm better I want to see that sunrise again, and I want to take you with me.'

I had the feeling he still did.

But the perilous, futile trail of recovery we'd been limping along together for years had left me depleted and confused. I'd morphed into an auto-pilot-crisis-management zombie with no time to process where and why it had all gone wrong, or head-space to write about it. Some form of reflective, healing journey might be the answer.

But was Peru, with its Conquistadors, Shining Path Maoist guerrillas and heartbreaking poverty a sensible choice? It had never been on my tourist radar. The country was, however, home to that most sacred – and visited –

site in Latin America, the site that Sacha most loved. So it would, quite simply, have to be.

Already, it was almost a year since he'd died, but was I brave enough yet to make the journey to Machu Picchu to scatter my son's ashes? I'd spent the last few years fending off my terror of death; now I was afraid of life. The tectonic plates of my world had imploded. I was in fragments. There was a permanent knot in my stomach – the severed umbilical cord.

All I knew was that I had to go soon. And that I had to go alone.

The funeral parlour was conveniently situated at the end of my road. Lee, the bulbous, balding undertaker who ran this 100-year-old family business, was expecting me. In our dealings to date, he'd shown a concern above and beyond the call of duty. Today there was a silent understanding between us: we both knew that, for me, what was about to take place would be deeply disturbing. Lee showed me into his office and pulled out a chair. I handed over the wooden urn and he left the room.

It's neither easy nor cheap to take the ashes of your beloved abroad. I'd had to send Sacha's death and cremation certificates to the Foreign and Commonwealth Office in London to be signed and stamped, at a cost of twenty pounds each. They kept all the money but returned only the death certificate. After hours of trying to get through to them on the phone, I finally learned that they hadn't stamped the cremation certificate because it wasn't signed by the crematorium registrar in person. I had to grit my teeth and return to the crematorium. Once the Foreign and Commonwealth Office had finally stamped and returned the new certificate, I was required to forward both certificates (and another forty pounds) to the Peruvian embassy to be stamped yet again.

That, however, proved to be the easy part. Because my flight would take me via the United States, I also had to contend with US regulations. After spending what seemed like a lifetime trying to get hold of the relevant official in the US embassy in London, I was told I couldn't take the casket containing the ashes through US security because it had a metal plaque on it; I'd have to take the ashes in an unsealed bag. This was what I had come to the undertaker's to collect.

Five minutes later, Lee returned, watery-eyed, and apologetically presented me with a nondescript plastic bag containing all that remained of my beautiful son. Had that powerful, vibrant energy that once constituted Sacha really metamorphosed into nothing more than a bag of gritty, grey dust? Even if I were a seasoned agnostic I'd find that hard to believe. Surely, such energy could never die?

Starlings circled overhead as I stumbled back up the road to my house, clutching the plastic bag to my chest, tears splattering the pavement. The postman who had delivered our mail for years propped his bike up against the wall and stared at me curiously. If he only knew that inside the plastic bag were the remains of that friendly young guy who kept a firm hold on those lively German Shepherds of his when he answered the door – drum 'n' bass blaring out from behind.

Once home, I knelt down on the living room floor. Steeling myself, I transferred the ashes into a hand-embroidered orange silk pouch and placed them inside the small, expensive, black leather rucksack I'd purchased for their transportation.

David, my partner of ten years, was in tears when he dropped me off at the airport.

'You don't have to get on that plane, you know. There's still time.

He was worried I wouldn't be strong enough to see it through – or worse, that I might not come back.

He looked exhausted. David worked in television news, and had been up all night editing. The last few years had been almost as testing for him as they had for me. Our marriage had been tested too, but it was the third for both of us and from its outset we were determined to make it work. Our Buddhist practice helped. I was grateful to David for never putting me in the position where I had to choose between him and Sacha.

'Promise you won't go mental on that motorbike,' I said, trying to deflect the threat of danger from myself. He nodded unconvincingly. Conscious that grief had made me more selfish, I hugged my husband goodbye and walked away.

On the flight from Gatwick to Atlanta, the stewardess insisted that my precious cargo be placed in the overhead locker. I tried to distract myself by wondering, as we flew over the wilderness of the Arctic, whether Sacha, too, could see the glaciers, the fjords and the intricate patterns of light dancing above Greenland's ice sheet. He'd had such a love of nature and, for that matter, of life. Strange really, as at birth he'd not wanted to make an appearance and had to be induced. A few weeks after he finally slid out, calmly and contentedly sucking his thumb, the health visitor made me take him to the doctor for a check-up because he almost never cried. I guess he was saving it up for later.

'Well, maaaam?' the American immigration official growled. 'Why *are* you travelling on your own to Peru?'

His glare remained fixed. To avoid further invasive questioning, I lied and said that my husband would be joining me at Christmas.

'That all your luggage?' he asked, pointing at the rucksack.

'I checked in a suitcase at Gatwick.'

He leafed through my passport.

'Employed?'

Again, I hesitated. Years earlier, when I worked as a performance artist, I'd been strip-searched and had my hand luggage torn apart at JFK International Airport for no apparent reason other than my unconventional occupation. Anxious that 'writer' might arouse suspicion, and not wanting my beloved son's precious ashes to be callously manhandled, I opted for 'psychotherapist' instead. He grunted and let me through. It can be useful, sometimes, having two professions.

For the world's busiest airport, Atlanta's cavernous

concourse was surprisingly devoid of passengers. As if to compensate, a regiment of television screens blasted out CNN in all directions: a trauma expert was explaining that the victims of Hurricane Katrina were still reeling from shock and would need counselling for years. News footage from the summer showing desperate New Orleanians bobbing up and down in the water, clutching their pets or clinging to the sides of rescue boats, uncomfortably mirrored my own inner landscape.

On the television screen above the red Formica bar, Condoleezza Rice was busy trying to convince the world that the CIA weren't engaging in torture off US soil. I ordered a large, expensive glass of Pinot Grigio.

Condoleezza was replaced, a few soundbites later, by John Lennon and the announcement that today was the 25th anniversary of his death. Archive footage of John and Yoko came on, accompanied, predictably, by the song 'Imagine'. I felt a pang of envy for Yoko. She got to share her grief with millions of empathic others, and collective global grieving had helped to keep John's memory alive. But perhaps she would have preferred her grief to be private and hidden away in a body-bag like mine.

'I'm sorry, but he has to remain in the bag in the chapel of rest,' Lee had gently explained before the funeral, handing me a box of tissues. 'Your boy was a user. It's Health and Safety who won't permit it, love, not me.'

I sipped my wine and imagined that 'my boy' was perched on the bar stool beside me, complaining, as usual, about American beer and George Bush. I ask him whether Peruvian beer was any better. He raises his glass. '*Sí Señora, muchísimo!*' He chuckles, and starts to brag about all the really cool pre-Columbian sites he is going to take me to…

A tannoy announced my flight to Lima. 'Get a grip!' I ordered myself as I gulped back the wine and headed for my gate. At the security barrier I was instructed to remove my shoes and join a short queue. I placed the rucksack in a tray and watched as a wheelchair-bound octogenarian lady was ordered to vacate her chair, remove her beige sling-backs and hobble through the security door. She was hardly your typical shoe-bomber. My paperwork was in order but my paranoia that they might want to examine the ashes – or, worse still, confiscate and test them for concealed drugs – resurfaced.

I began fighting my own war against terror: the thought of a stranger sifting through the delicate remains of my beloved son made my stomach heave. Fortunately for me, the old lady's distress distracted the guard monitoring the security screen. He barely glanced at the interior of my rucksack and the ashes made it through.

As the Lima-bound plane took off into the funky gloom of Georgia, the atmosphere started to feel lighter. Spanish was being spoken all around me. Keen to refresh mine, I eavesdropped on conversations, but struggled to keep up. The seat next to me was empty. That's Sacha's seat, I thought to myself. I closed my eyes and pictured him sat beside me, his warm arm, with its neat Celtic tattoo and tarnished silver bracelets, nestling against mine.

As we approached the southern hemisphere, a slender magnolia moon appeared above the wing of the plane. Beyond it, a smattering of stars lit up the indigo sky. I remembered Sacha telling me the Incas believed each star was the protector of a particular species of animal or bird, and that, for these mysterious people, the dark shapeless voids which existed between the constellations held more symbolic meaning than the constellations themselves. I pressed my face to the window and examined the night sky. Would I ever be able to find meaning in the dark, shapeless void which had engulfed my own life? I wanted to get closer to my son on this trip, closer to his world. Wherever and whatever it was now.

We landed in Lima around midnight. As the queue inched its way towards immigration I chatted with a woman from Alabama who was on my flight. She'd been working for the Internal Revenue Service (the US tax department) for more than fifteen years, she told me. Dressed from head to toe in denim with a badge-strewn straw hat pulled tightly over her chilli-red hair, she was, she said, intending to spend the night in the airport before taking an early morning flight to Iquitos. There she would meet up with a group of like-minded travellers and continue for several more hours by bus and boat deep into the Amazon jungle for a week-long inner journey where they would ingest *ayahuasca* at a shamanic retreat.

*Ayahuasca* was, she explained, a concoction made from hallucinogenic Amazonian plants. She hoped it would purge her of a toxic relationship from which she'd recently escaped and revamp her stagnant life.

While admiring her courage, I couldn't help wondering whether quitting her job and exploring Peru itself might be a better way of achieving the life change she was seeking than this week-long quick fix with, perhaps, a dose of dengue fever thrown in. But I kept my mouth shut. Deep down, I was hoping that Peru would fix me.

Reunited with my suitcase, I found myself in yet another buttock-clenching airport queue. A customs official with an elaborately coiffeured beehive presided over a barrier above which there were two lights. I watched as she scrutinised each passenger then paused for several moments, like a sadistic game-show hostess, before pressing the button to illuminate either the red or the green light. On the other side of the barrier I could see the unfortunate 'reds' having their luggage torn apart by guys in military uniform.

It was my turn. Might all that remained of my darling Sacha be pawed, prodded around or even taken away by those stern-faced soldiers? Fear rampaged inside me as I looked her in the eye. She stared back and pressed the green light. Dizzy with relief, I lurched through the barrier. The taxi driver, sent courtesy of my pre-booked hotel, ran over and grabbed my suitcase.

As we sped along El Paseo de la República in the early hours of the morning, Lima was as wide awake as me. As for my skinny young driver – well, he too was clearly adrenaline-fuelled, his driving frenzied and haphazard. Pizarro had daringly constructed his sprawling Ciudad de los Reyes – City of the Kings – on a quake-prone desert. I wound down the window and breathed in the sultry night air; I could smell the Pacific Ocean. Already I sensed that Peru would prove to be a land rich in culture and mystery.

The lively driver chattered incessantly, turning the car around to point out tastefully illuminated palaces, basilicas, fountains and *haute cuisine* eateries. I admired the mixture of stately colonial and ultra-modern architecture that he pointed out in this impromptu whirlwind tour, but turned down his offer to drive me around the *barriadas* (slum districts) which, he informed me, had been euphemistically re-named *pueblos jóvenes* (young towns).

He eventually dropped me off outside my hotel, El Balcón Dorado, collected the complimentary pick-up fare from the weary-looking proprietor and accelerated off into the night. I suspected that his frenetic driving and effervescent commentary might have been fuelled by a touch of the indigenous joy powder.

The Golden Balcony – to render my hotel's name in English – was yet another of those scruffy establishments that had looked great on the internet. But I was too tired to care. A sleepy-eyed lady holding a wide-awake toddler welcomed me. She introduced herself as Martha, the proprietor's wife, and handed me a drink which resembled a Margarita. It was, she explained, a Pisco Sour – a white grape brandy from the port of Pisco, mixed with lime juice, egg white and Angostura bitters. It tasted divine.

My room, I was surprised to discover, came with a reasonably sized ante-room stuffed with Euro-posh repro furniture, including a fake Napoleonic *chaise longue* and

23

a pair of Swiss mountain prints, framed ornately in gold plastic. I couldn't help but smile. At the very least I'd expected a print of the High Andes or an adobe Inca ruin or two. But never knowing quite where you might sleep or what you might be sleeping on was, for me, an intriguing – and challenging – aspect of travel.

The room itself was pretty basic. A narrow partition led to a minuscule *en-suite*, comprising a rusty hand shower, a tiny basin and a creaky old loo. Compared to some of the mosquito-ridden bucket-bath lodges in Africa in which I'd stayed over the years, this was luxury. And situated on the corner of Lima's Plaza Mayor, the historic heart of the city, El Balcón Dorado was about as central as I could get. After a tepid shower I flopped onto a lumpy old mattress and fell into a deep, dreamless sleep.

# señor ruiz

## finding the courage

Over breakfast the next morning I dipped into my Peru guide but, flickering through its pages, the weariness of indecision descended upon me. Until two days earlier, this trip was going to be simple, so very simple. In November, I'd booked my month-long, non-refundable ticket, flying out to Lima in early December. I'd intended to go directly from the capital to Cusco, the launch pad for Machu Picchu. Once I'd scattered Sacha's ashes, my plan was to collapse in some tranquil, grief-friendly resort near the sea for the remainder of my stay, and chill.

Then Roberto called.

Roberto was my ex-husband. To my surprise, he told me he wanted to attend the scattering – but insisted he couldn't make it to Peru until the end of December. His trip, he pointed out, would coincide with the first anniversary of

Sacha's death on 2nd January. Roberto was the last person in the world I felt like meeting up with. But he was also Sacha's father, and I couldn't deny him the right to be present.

I hadn't seen him since the funeral – nor had I wanted to. Although he loved his son, I suspected that Roberto, the partner in a Franco-Colombian architectural practice, had deliberately chosen to run its Africa office from Lagos to maintain a convenient distance between himself and Sacha's troubles. I was still angry with him for that.

In my heart, however, I knew the timing made sense. Perhaps Sacha himself wanted his ashes to be scattered on the first anniversary of his death by his mother *and* his father.

The prospect of being holed up in a hotel for nearly a month waiting for Roberto to arrive was grim, but did I have the courage to hit the road – with the ashes in tow – and explore Peru alone? In a complete quandary, I ventured out to change some traveller's cheques.

Ten minutes after leaving El Balcón Dorado, I was lost. The street names bore no resemblance to those on my map and Friday's bank queues were snaking around the plazas. I was thirsty, but without any sol – the local currency – I couldn't even buy a bottle of water, let alone grab a taxi back to the jet-lag sanctuary of the hotel. With its loud Latin jazz, traffic horns and growling street dogs, daytime Lima was certainly as lively and chaotic as I'd anticipated, and scary too: my guide book warned of 'strangle muggers' who roamed the streets, throttling and robbing unsuspecting tourists.

A robust young policeman strode over and asked me if I was lost. He offered to escort me to the Plaza Mayor where, he claimed, the banks weren't so busy. I didn't like to tell him that the Plaza Mayor was where I'd just come from.

When I'd last visited South America I was constantly quizzed about the Queen, but this young man showered me with questions about that new British royal: Wayne Rooney. To keep him at my side for as long as possible, I dredged up all the superlative adjectives about Wayne and the Premier League my wobbly Spanish could muster, until we arrived at the end of his patch – and back at El Balcón Dorado.

An hour later I plucked up the courage to venture out again. Wandering down a narrow pedestrian side street, I stopped to admire a Spanish colonial building of glistening white marble. Amazingly, it was a bank; a cool, empty, queue-less bank with a good exchange rate. Sunlight streamed in through the glass-domed ceiling. I felt a quick pang of excitement as the friendly cashier counted out my sol: I'd actually made it to Peru.

The cashier volunteered advice on what to see in Lima. Sightseeing was a great idea: it meant I could delay having to make a decision about what to do next.

The yellow stucco façade of the baroque Monastery of San Francisco was almost obscured by the sea of pigeons that swarmed around it – courtesy of the vendors selling bags of seed at its gates. To avoid the grungy flock I headed straight down a flight of steps and into the crypt.

This was a big mistake: skulls and femurs, meticulously arranged into neat concentric circles, reminiscent of the worst excesses of Pol Pot, gazed back at me. Over the last few centuries, these bone-filled, candlelit catacombs had witnessed some 70,000 burials. Someone coughed. I gasped. They jumped. A woman emerged from the shadows. We both laughed, relieved not to be alone in this subterranean cemetery. The woman, who was Dutch, told me it was her last day in Peru; I replied that it was my first. She said she envied me. I smiled and made my escape.

Blinking away sunlight, I hurried through a terracotta passageway lined with red geraniums into a cool, verdant courtyard surrounded by white, arched cloisters. My eyes alighted on a fading wall mural of a 16th-century monk in the act of licking the leg of a leper. Perhaps this reckless gesture of humility explained some of those dry old bones down below.

Heavy with tapestries, the monastery also housed a library of antique texts dating back to the Conquistadors, and its mainly Peruvian art collection also included a Rubens and a Van Dyck. I stared, transfixed, at an 18th-century Pietà image of Mary cradling the body of her dead son. Jesus! How that iconic image resonated. My mind flitted back to a summer in Rome three years earlier. I had been in St Peter's, staring at Michelangelo's version of the Pietà. The image of a mother holding her dead son was my worst fear crystallised in stone. Back then, it was still only a fear.

My eyes welled up yet again. Over the preceding year, man-size Kleenex and waterproof mascara had become my constant companions. The thick, curly, luxuriant hair, pale skin and large, soulful, grey-green eyes of the Christ in this painting bore a striking resemblance to my handsome son. Sacha was no Jesus, and I'd been a Buddhist for over twenty years, but I couldn't help thinking that Mary and I had quite a bit in common.

As I walked out of San Francisco's gates, a couple of shoeless street boys ran over. The elder of the two was wearing a torn, faded Manchester United shirt several sizes too big for him. They wanted to sell me a dog-eared postcard of Lima. I gave them some coins and told them to keep the card, but in a touching display of dignity they insisted I take it. These lads tore at my heartstrings. Instead of flowers at Sacha's funeral, I'd asked for donations to be made to a foundation for Colombian street kids.

I realised, too late, that the nearby restaurant I'd dived into was full of wealthy Chinese who could afford its astronomical prices. I ordered a beer and the national dish of *ceviche*, a concoction of raw sea fish marinated in lemon and lime juice. Sacha had told me that Limeños took their food very seriously, and claimed it was the best cuisine in Latin America – if not the world. I found myself wondering what he'd made of the *ceviche* when he had been in Peru eight years earlier.

Sacha had to spend several weeks in Lima because his passport and traveller's cheques were stolen. At the time, I was in the Czech Republic, where there was no phone signal. American Express refused to replace the cheques until I'd verified his identity. I didn't pick up Sacha's calls until two weeks later.

He'd managed to survive, he later told me, because

friends he'd made in Lima held a benefit for him. Whether it took place in an upmarket eatery like this or in a corrugated shack in the *barriadas*, I hadn't a clue. It could have been either. He befriended people from all walks of life (unless they happened to be an authority figure or wore a uniform). For Sacha, being with almost anyone was preferable to being alone and at the mercy of the voices inside his head.

Back at El Balcón Dorado later that evening, I was in for a heart-stopping moment when I opened the door to my room. The bed had been made but my suitcase, containing my valuables, was lying brazenly unzipped in the middle of the floor. Trembling, I looked inside. Everything was still there, untouched, including my traveller's cheques. What an idiot! It was so unlike me, a seasoned traveller, to be so negligent. An early night was imperative. I hurried to a scruffy-looking café around the corner. Under cruel fluorescent lighting and the deafening screams and applause of non-Premier League football, I feasted, this time, on fried chicken, chips and Coca-Cola.

Prising open my hotel window I stared down at the stationary, toxic traffic below. The weather was damp, cloudy and cool – an unwelcome change from the sunshine of the day before. After waking up from a grief-laden dream and still incapable of making a decision about what I should do for the next month, my most sensible option, I realised, was to grab a cab and head for the Buddhist centre.

Hernan, the affable driver of the battered old Ford taxi I hailed, looked devastated when the vehicle conked out thirty seconds into the journey, at a ferocious rush-hour junction. I had the feeling that this happened to him many times, on a daily basis, and that he was more concerned about losing my fare than with the deafening crescendo of angry horns. I got out and helped him push-start the car.

We managed, at last, to locate the Buddhist centre behind a high wall in the leafy, posh ambassadorial neighbourhood in the suburb of San Isidro. I pressed the entry phone. No answer. I glanced at my watch. It was still only eight o'clock.

To kill time before the centre opened we drove to the Huaca Pucllana – a massive pre-Inca adobe ruin nearby – but that, too, was closed. We drove on to the coastline at Miraflores, where the sea mist was so dense I couldn't see the sea. A wet, listless hour later we returned to the centre, only to find it was still closed. I felt a powerful surge of frustration; I needed to ground myself in Peru.

Hernan tried his hardest to convince me, as we headed back towards the city centre, that (for a substantial number of sol) I should let him spend the rest of the day driving me around the sights of Lima. We passed a vast concrete heap of a building, so hideous it made London's National Theatre look like the Alhambra Palace. I feigned interest when he told me it was the National Museum, and asked him to drop me off there. He smiled at me wistfully as we went our separate ways.

Once inside, I headed for the top floor where there was an exhibition of ancient Peruvian gold artefacts. The spacious room I entered was completely dark and empty apart from a few illuminated exhibits of gold masks and trinkets. A museum guard in a green uniform insisted on following me around so closely I could feel his breath on the back of my neck.

When the Conquistadors arrived in Peru, Quechua was the official language of the Inca Empire which was, at that time, the largest empire in the world. The guard told me his name was Ernesto, and that he was of Quechua descent – and proudly so. We chatted away in Spanish for a bit, then he asked me how old I thought he was. Ernesto was forty-five if he was a day – so I said thirty-five to be polite. He informed me – in all seriousness – that he was twenty-seven, and insisted on accompanying me all the way down multiple flights of stairs to the ground floor. We shook hands and he asked me for *uno besito* (a little kiss). I laughed and exclaimed, '*Hombre! No!*'

Downstairs, along with a handful of Latinos and Gringos, I was coaxed into joining the guided museum tour led by a Señor Ruiz. This bilingual, bespectacled thirty-something guide had an extremely commanding voice – and no arms. He operated a torch with his teeth to illuminate designs on ancient Chavín and Nazca ceramics, and used his foot to draw explanatory diagrams of Moche pyramids and Wari sand settlements. His fascinating archaeological observations were interspersed with bouts of boyish, high-pitched giggling.

A couple from Ohio with teenage kids drifted away from the group when he told us that the Incas saw nothing wrong with having loads of sex, and then accused the Catholic

Church of messing people's heads up over the centuries with its repressive morality. So he was brave, too. From what I'd heard about Peru, it was a deeply religious country. An outspoken comment like that could cost Señor Ruiz his job.

I was riveted by the sheer energy of his performance – and by his humour. If he could triumph so cheerfully and unselfconsciously over his disability, surely I could summon up the nerve to get out of Lima and see something of Peru?

Over lunch in the museum café, I made a few calls and managed to get hold of the number of the Buddhist centre in San Isidro. A warm voice answered the phone and assured me that the centre was now open. I quickly finished my food and hailed a cab at the museum entrance.

Behind the impenetrably high wall at last, I was greeted by Oscar – a chubby young *mestizo* (a person of mixed Spanish and Quechan ancestry) with sparkling brown eyes. He showed me around the spacious centre, where the utilitarian vibe was partially redeemed by an elegantly paved courtyard decked out with purple bougainvilleas and dwarf palms. The centre was part of the priest-free, socially engaged movement known as Soka Gakkai. Based on the teachings of the 13th-century Buddhist teacher Nichiren, the movement believes in the universality of Buddhahood, and is a powerful peace movement and a United Nations NGO. As in all its centres around the world, there wasn't an orange robe or a shaven head in sight.

At my request, Oscar led me to the large, high-ceilinged

chanting hall, which contained several hundred fold-up chairs – and not a single person. For two hours I sat alone before the altar and chanted to the Peru Gohonzon: a mandala inscribed in black ink on a golden scroll that depicted in Sanskrit and ancient Chinese all the workings of life and the universe.

As I chanted, I remembered some of Sacha's fearless – and foolhardy – exploits in South America, such as travelling into the FARC guerrilla region in Colombia, a hotbed of kidnapping, to look for ancient Mayan ruins. Then I thought about the monks who never strayed from the cloisters of San Francisco monastery, and of all the dried-up old bones lining the catacombs. And in my heart, I knew that Sacha would want me to see Peru. In fact, with his love of the continent, he would smile and pronounce it 'wicked' that his ashes would be travelling around the country with me.

Emboldened by this resolve, I made my way to Lima bus station, where I purchased a Royal Coach ticket to Cusco, with open stopping-off points on the way, on a coach departing the following morning. Then, in a retro travel agency near La Plaza Mayor, which had reams of carbon paper but not a computer or photocopier in sight, a young man called Luis spent nearly an hour on the phone booking my flight from Cusco back to Lima. His blond highlights and earring-drooped earlobe were refreshingly out of place in the antediluvian agency. Outside, a noisy demonstration of people yelling '*Bastante! Bastante! Bastante!*' passed by.

I wondered what it was they'd had 'enough' of. '*Izquierdo*

*o derecho?'* I asked Luis, curious to know whether the protesters were left-wing or right.

'*Centro derecho,'* he replied. Centre-right.

I took out my camera, hurried into the street and began snapping away. A jack-booted police officer in a dark grey uniform and matching baseball cap, clutching a riot shield, sprinted over to me and shook his baton in my face. I put my camera away and sloped off, reminding myself that sometimes I could be just as foolhardy as Sacha.

Before leaving Lima there was something I wanted to see. The cathedral was just around the corner from El Balcón Dorado, and inside it was Pizarro's tomb. The brightly coloured mosaic above his regal chapel neatly depicted the triumphs of Atahualpa's murderer: in the foreground, in full armour, Pizarro prayed with a clothed, converted Inca, while behind him a handful of Conquistadors herded naked Incas onto a rowing boat to be shipped off to Spain in an enormous galleon, its white sails billowing on the horizon.

I planted myself on a pew to admire the cathedral's voluptuous interior. Like their erstwhile Spanish conquerors, the Peruvians appeared to prefer sculptured mannequins in their churches to religious pictures. But the mannequins in this cathedral were unlike the grisly, bloodied, Madame Tussaud-style effigies I'd seen in Spanish churches. I gazed up in wonder at glittering life-sized Madonnas in ball gowns and virile, handsome young Christs.

Glancing up at the altar, I discovered that I'd unwittingly become one of a congregation of eight. An elderly bishop in purple robes, aided by a young priest, was about to begin Mass. Reluctant to reduce the bishop's minuscule flock even further, I resigned myself to sitting it out. As the Mass murmured on, I watched a couple of baby-faced novices nervously dust the religious artefacts behind the altar. As a child, Sacha, too, had choirboy good looks. Would he still be alive, I wondered, if he'd been ugly?

The Mass ended and I made my way out of the dimly lit cathedral. It was Pizarro who had carried, on his shoulder, the first log to be used in the construction of the cathedral, and had laid its first stone. As I exited through the Portada del Perdón I hoped that, in an act of contrition, it was the treasure-thief himself who had named it the Gate of Forgiveness.

# in the desert

## the fear factor

'No one ever told me that grief felt so like fear,' the bereaved writer CS Lewis observed. For the previous three years my fear had focused on Sacha and keeping him alive, but by the time I set out to explore Peru, its spotlight was well and truly on me. Sometimes this shadowy travelling companion got the better of me, but not always – as I was soon to discover on the Pan-American Highway.

I'd checked my suitcase in at an airport-style desk in Lima bus station, found myself a seat by the departure bay and awaited the arrival of my 9am Royal double-decker coach to the town of Ica, my first stopping-off point en route to Cusco.

A couple of Peruvian guys setting off on their Christmas break warned me the coaches were always late. I waited an hour and then returned to the desk, where I was informed that I should have got on the 9am coach to La Paz, which went via Ica. Now they tell me! The unsympathetic girl at the desk insisted it was my fault and that I'd have to buy another ticket and take the next coach at 1pm. I was about to protest when it suddenly hit me: my suitcase – stuffed with clothes, books, toiletries, iPod, camera and jewellery (I never travel light) – was on its way to Bolivia.

At my insistence the girl called the Ica bus station but wasn't able to get through, and casually remarked that it was probably the wrong number anyway. I scribbled it down and stormed out. There was nothing else for it but to find a taxi to drive me hell-for-leather to Ica and attempt to rescue my case when the coach pulled into the station.

Outside, a rabble of cabbies crowded around. Sensing my desperation they demanded absurd money – in US dollars. One promised he'd take me to Ica for $100. We shook on it, but my heart sank when I saw that his taxi looked as old and dodgy as he did. On the outskirts of Lima he suddenly stopped the engine, swung around in his seat and told me $100 wasn't enough; he wanted $200. I got out.

A few minutes later a newer-looking taxi with a younger driver pulled up. I explained my predicament and, after some good-natured haggling, we agreed on $150. His smile seemed sincere, and the oversized St Christopher medallion dangling from his windscreen mirror reassuring. But the surge of relief I felt as the car sped away was premature; ten minutes later we hit a traffic jam that held us up for an hour.

Once we were finally on the Peruvian section of the Pan-American Highway, the 48,000-kilometre network of roads linking the mainland countries of the Americas, it was pretty obvious there was no way we'd make what was a four-hour journey by coach in only two.

After several attempts I managed to get through by phone to a bus station official in Ica and begged him to take my case off the coach when it arrived. The line kept breaking up and my clumsy Spanish became increasingly neurotic as I struggled to describe the nondescript case's only distinguishing feature – the plastic orange address tag I'd hastily purchased at Gatwick airport three days earlier. Then the line went dead.

The driver, who hadn't said a word since we'd been on the highway, pulled into a service station and told me that if I didn't give him $50 for petrol he'd have to return to Lima. I had little choice but to pay up. We'd be travelling companions for a few hours more, so I bought us soft drinks and cakes. Noticing a faded family photograph taped to his dashboard, I asked him about his wife and kids. His responses were so monosyllabic I gave up.

Half an hour later, even though the petrol gauge was showing a full tank, he swerved into another petrol station and again demanded $50. I itched to tell him he was a complete and utter *coño*, but I couldn't risk it. He went through the motions of filling up, then disappeared into the toilet, while I wandered around the dusty forecourt, fuming. I thought of David back in England. This was exactly the sort of scenario he'd dreaded.

A long greenish snake with yellow markings was sliding down a disused pump. I knew there were plenty of boa constrictors and anacondas in Peru, but I was unable to identify this one. Sacha and I shared an interest in reptiles, although we both knew they weren't to everybody's liking. Once, we were in a train compartment with two old ladies. In a mischievous mood, Sacha, then aged nine, took his pet garter snake Sid out of his inside blazer pocket and let it slither all over him. One of the women screamed for the guard.

Later, as a temperamental teenager, unbeknown to me, he kept a pet white rat in a drawer in his bedroom and, according to the teacher who complained, would take it out of his pocket in lessons. An act of rebellion, I suppose. The little bugger knew I had a rat phobia.

The driver honked the horn and I hurried back to the car, wishing I'd had the courage to pick the snake up and wrap it around his steering wheel.

Three hours into the four-hour journey through barren wasteland and interminable sand dunes, the driver stopped and asked me a third time for petrol money. Now he wanted $100. Trying to appeal to his better nature I tearfully explained that I was in Peru to scatter my son's ashes. He shrugged his shoulders and insisted we were going nowhere until I handed over more money. We'd hardly passed anything or anyone on the barren highway – only a few deserted-looking shacks for *los pobres* sprinkled amongst the dunes.

My imagination went into overdrive: he could easily force me out of the car and drive back to Lima – or worse still, cut my throat and dump my body in the desert. I 'heard'

Sacha whisper in my head, 'It's alright Mum, it's going to be alright,' but I still wasn't convinced it was going to be alright. The last time I'd felt this concerned for my safety was when a drugs cartel issued a death sentence on every member of my son's Colombian family.

Jaime, Sacha's cousin, had been working undercover for the US Drugs Enforcement Agency (DEA). No one – least of all his family – knew he was being paid millions of pesos to infiltrate the cartel. When Sacha visited Colombia, Jaime met him at the airport in an armoured truck accompanied by his bodyguards. During his visit they would drive to luxurious *haciendas* belonging to Jaime's wealthy '*amigos*'. Sacha played chess and drank *aguardiente* – Colombian firewater – with these guys without ever knowing they were infamous drug barons.

Then, out of the blue, Jaime's cover was blown and the cartel issued a death sentence on every member of his family. Overnight, brothers, sisters, aunts, uncles, cousins and even Sacha's poor grandmother, who was suffering from osteoporosis, were flown to Florida under the protection of the DEA and given new identities. It was like something out of the 1980s TV series *Miami Vice*. This was no idle death threat. Life then (as now) was cheap in Colombia, and the people hungry. Kids as young as ten years old would charge a dollar per assassination.

Roberto rang me in London to warn me that, as we were 'family' and still shared the same incriminating surname, we could be contacted. A few days later a guy with a

Colombian accent called and asked for Roberto. It was the voice of a killer. He knew my phone number. Maybe he knew my address too. I lied and said I hadn't seen Roberto since our divorce years earlier. Thankfully, Sacha was away at the time. Feeling unsafe on my own, I fled to a friend's empty holiday home in Cornwall. Although I had a deadline to meet for a writing commission, I was too anxious to work.

One day, marooned by rain in a little chapel along the coast, bored and lonely, an intense rage welled up in me: how the hell had I allowed my life, my creativity, to be sabotaged by psychopathic scumbags living thousands of miles away? My fear vanished and I caught the next train home.

Now, in the back of the sweltering cab, driving through the barren desert, my fear once again turned to anger. Fuck the driver. I had no choice but to hand the money over a third time but I made up my mind there was no way he was getting a cent out of me in Ica. I was going to make it to Machu Picchu, with or without the suitcase. Next to me on the back seat was the rucksack containing my passport, tickets, traveller's cheques and – most important of all – Sacha's ashes. I could do without everything else.

As soon as we hit the first set of red traffic lights in Ica I jumped out of the taxi. When the driver protested, I icily informed him that I'd taken down his licence number, and threatened him with the police. The lights turned green and he had no choice but to drive on.

Inside Ica bus station a middle-aged transport official looked up at me from behind a desk and slowly clapped his hands.

'*Aha, la chica sin la maleta. Dios mio!*'

He pointed to my solitary case propped up behind the grubby counter, its little plastic orange tag smiling at me. I wept tears of relief.

Half an hour later, sipping a complimentary Pisco Sour on the veranda of my hotel overlooking a lagoon in the oasis village of Huacachina, I was feeling pretty smug. Not only had I survived the Pan-American Highway, I'd also managed to negotiate a fantastic off-peak week-long deal at the half-empty hotel. And, according to my guide book, this 'elegant and luxurious' establishment was the very best in the oasis. I marvelled at how travel can sometimes catapult you from hell into paradise in the space of minutes.

My spacious room in the Hotel Mossone was in a one-storey annexe built around an elegant, arched garden courtyard offering panoramic views of mountainous sand dunes. With its parquet floors and bright upholstery, the room had a homely ambience. I found a small combination safe in the wardrobe and placed Sacha's ashes inside; they just fitted. I felt relieved we'd both found a comfortable base for a week.

That evening, at an internet café beside the lagoon, Victor the waiter – an elderly Picasso-lookalike – brought over the menu, pulled up a chair and started to chat. I learnt that he was the owner's brother, and had come down from Pisco to help out in preparation for the Christmas holiday rush. His manner was kindly and avuncular. After the harrowing events of the day a touch of human warmth was more than

43

welcome. A smoke would have been more than welcome, too.

Victor was curious to know why I was travelling *'sola, sin esposo'*. It felt right somehow to tell him why I'd come to Peru alone, without my husband.

His eyes welled up in sympathy. *'La vida es tan difficil,'* he sighed.

I asked him if he could sell me a cigarillo. I'd started smoking them again on the night of Sacha's funeral as a sort of grief displacement, but had stopped a month before leaving, in preparation for the climbing I was anticipating I'd have to do here. He returned with a couple of fags and patiently explained that they didn't have cigarillos in Peru. They never quite do it for me – cigarettes – but I took one anyway.

As I watched the cigarette smoke float over the still lagoon I recalled how I'd 'heard' Sacha whisper in my head 'It's alright, Mum, it's going to be alright' when I was panicking in the desert that afternoon. This wasn't the first time since his death that he'd 'whispered' to me. Sacha communicated with me when *he* wanted to – not when *I* wanted him to. That much hadn't changed.

On my second day in the oasis, I watched with envy as elderly Peruvians rolled around in the mud and sand on the lagoon's palm-shaded banks, and energetic backpackers surfed the lunar dunes that surrounded it. The lagoon's alleged curative powers for arthritis, rheumatism and asthma had, in the 1940s, transformed the oasis into an exclusive resort. Politicians, diplomats and film stars stayed in the Mosonne and listened to concerts on its colonial-style veranda. How I wished, as I stared into its murky waters, that the lagoon's curative powers also extended to diarrhoea.

I had only myself to blame for this unwelcome affliction. Eagerly anticipating my naughty nicotine hit at Victor's, I'd taken my eye off the ball and glanced only briefly at the menu before ordering a Russian salad with my omelette – definitely a no-no in countries with questionable water. I'd travelled enough to know that. After leaving the restaurant I'd stopped to ask a local sandboarding instructor about lessons. Suddenly, in mid conversation, I had to make an embarrassing dash back to the hotel – leaving the poor guy wondering what on earth it was he'd said to me.

Not daring to stray far from my room, it wasn't long before the oasis began to feel like a luxurious prison of fermenting grief. A couple of friends back home had talked about my going to Peru for 'the peace and rest you deserve'. Those friends, I decided, didn't really understand how grief worked. It was anything but peaceful.

I woke up at dawn one morning, overcome with sadness after yet another Sacha dream: I see him from the back, cycling down the hill where he lived in Brighton, wearing his trademark baseball cap. Running after the bike, I call, 'Sacha! Sacha! Stop! Stop!' The bike screeches to a halt and he turns around slowly to face me. But it isn't Sacha. It's a woman who tells me that the bike and cap used to belong to Sacha; now they're hers.

I climbed out of bed and looked through the small barred

window. In the distance I could hear drunken shouting. A rooster was crowing and a few chickens were pecking at a patch of grass outside. Solitary Peruvians ambled to work, unaware they were being watched as they combed their hair and picked their noses. How ultimately alone we all are, I thought. I unlocked the safe and took out the ashes. They felt cold, yet warm.

I'd read in a magazine that after the drug-fuelled 'suicide' of her rock-star partner Michael Hutchence, writer and TV presenter Paula Yates sewed her lover's ashes into a pillow and found comfort sleeping with them under her head. As I drifted back off to sleep with the ashes on the pillow beside me, I recalled an afternoon, shortly before Hutchence's fatal trip to Australia, when Sacha and I bumped into them both on the King's Road in Chelsea.

We were in search of a tapas bar when Paula, with Hutchence in tow, stopped in her tracks in front of me. I was wearing dark glasses and what, I guess, at the time, was a pretty chic red coat. She smiled at me radiantly and asked me how I was.

Yates, with her ice-blonde hair, Monroe lips and Prada dress, looked as if she'd stepped off the cover of *Harpers & Queen*. Hutchence, on the other hand, could have just crawled off the mattress of a Brixton squat. I smiled and told Paula that she must have mistaken me for someone else. We'd never met. She insisted that she knew me, and that we'd danced together at some party in St John's Wood the week before.

This silly conversation continued for a couple of minutes until Hutchence took off his shades and yawned and Sacha began tugging at my arm.

'Has she lost it or have I?' I asked Sacha as we walked away.

'She's on heroin, Mum. They both are. Their eyes are pinned.'

'Pinned?'

'The pupils shrink to tiny dots when you're on skag.'

'How do you know, Sacha?' I snapped.

'A girl I went to school with shoots up.'

Not long after Hutchence's death, Yates died of a heroin overdose. It was chilling to think that all three of them were now dead. And I didn't know then, as I slept in Huacachina with the ashes beside me, that heroin would one day claw its way into a future generation and tragically claim the life of Paula's daughter as well.

I woke up and wandered out onto the sun-dappled courtyard. A giant tortoise sauntered up to me. I started talking to him in English then switched to Spanish. The cleaners close by laughed. They told me his name was Pedro and that he was thirty – Sacha's age when he died. I'd given birth to him when I was twenty. Too young, I thought, to be a mother – especially such an emotionally immature one. I'd loathed my all-girls' grammar school and had left it – and home – at sixteen. But by the time I met Roberto I'd gained a few A-levels and was eager to get a degree.

David was also a father at twenty. He'd hastily married and joined the police force to support his young family. I, on the other hand, went to university, left Roberto, and took Sacha to the south of France to live with my then boyfriend, where I made and sold jewellery on the Côte d'Azur. For a time we lived in Montmartre in Paris, before returning to London, where I went to drama school. As much as I adored my little boy, I was a pretty self-centred young mum.

One of the cleaners wandered over and remarked that the *tortuga gigante* had taken a liking to me. I found it comforting, tickling Pedro's scrawny old chin. Later on, as the oasis had no mobile signal, I dragged myself up a dune hill to text David. I was starting to miss his gentle, loving, laid-back presence and wanted to thank him for putting together a great selection of iPod music for my trip.

I looked nervously at my call register: the last time I'd checked it was a month after Sacha's death, when it had shown multiple missed calls from him during the weeks prior to his death. DELETE SACHA? DELETE SACHA? a screen message asked over and over again. I'd never realised technology could be so cruel.

This time there were multiple missed calls from David but no voice message, only a text. He hadn't heard from me for a couple of days and sensed, correctly, that I wasn't feeling too good. He asked me to email him immediately.

Victor's place appeared to be the only functioning

internet café in the oasis, but I felt shy about seeing him again. It was more than just shyness; there was a feeling of dread that I'd grown accustomed to over the last year – an unfamiliar self-consciousness and lack of confidence, born of my bereavement. Had I said too much to Victor the other night? I was feeling so emotional after my taxi ordeal. No. I was getting paranoid. The bereaved need to talk: 'Give sorrow words,' says Malcolm to Macduff in *Macbeth*. 'The grief that does not speak, knits up the o'er wrought heart and bids it break.'

As I set off for the internet café, I realised what I was really afraid of: that Victor might pity me. My pride, I suppose. Compassion and empathy I accepted with gratitude, but who wants to be pitied?

The café was busy and Victor was rushed off his feet. He looked at me with gentle eyes, kissed me paternally and led me to an internet booth. The computer was so old and worn that I could hardly read the letters on the keyboard. An American backpacker with sand in his beard and lagoon mud on his legs was sitting at the computer next to mine. He and his poncho were in dire need of a wash. I wrote one of my quickest emails ever.

Still too weak to venture out of the oasis I spent the days lounging around the pool, which, most of the time, I had to myself. One afternoon, a couple of little girls wearing grubby *chullos* and sand-stained dresses shouted 'Gringo! Gringo!' and pulled faces at me from behind the high chicken-wire fence enclosing the pool. I made faces back and they giggled. The security guard shook his head when I tried to let them into the enclosure.

Compared to these kids Sacha had such a privileged childhood. As the first son of the first son, he was pampered by his wealthy Colombian relatives. I was frequently broke and couldn't afford to lavish gifts on him but Roberto, like many divorced dads who don't see their kids often, certainly could. He would take Sacha barracuda fishing in the South Atlantic Ocean and fly him to New York on Concorde. Once, he bought him a snooker table that barely fitted into our London living room.

I let myself out of the pool enclosure and gave the girls my untouched sandwich and bag of corn chips. They told me they lived in Ica and that their mother washed clothes for people in the oasis. Their own, I thought, must be the exception. At least they looked reasonably well fed and weren't polishing shoes or selling tat to tourists. The girls shook their heads when I asked if they went to school.

Sending Sacha away to school at the age of eight is my greatest regret in life. He was five years old when it became apparent that something wasn't right with the way he was seeing words and numbers. Two ophthalmic specialists and an educational psychologist later, he was diagnosed with dyslexia. This wasn't such a recognised condition in the 1980s, and there was limited help available in his state primary school. Finally, his father offered to pay for a private school. A couple of people close to me managed to convince me it would be in Sacha's best interest and my own.

I guess my guilt comes from that bit of me that colluded with this decision. I'd been dealing with the responsibility of motherhood from a young age, much of it alone, and now my performance work in the theatre was starting to take off, with the opportunity of touring abroad. I let myself be persuaded. We chose a boarding prep school with a dyslexia unit situated on the South Coast.

Behind the poolside bar of the Hotel Mossone, the *Rocky* theme tune, 'Eye Of The Tiger', blared out from a transistor radio that only played pre-1990 American pop music. It was the first single Sacha ever bought, and he played it over and over again, along with *The Wall* by Pink Floyd. That combination just about summed up his teenage years: pugilism and, like me, a hatred of school.

Memories, I couldn't take any more. I dragged myself up from the lounger and flopped into the pool. When I'd had to call the crematorium to request a signed cremation certificate for the Foreign and Commonwealth Office to stamp for this trip, I'd broken down in tears. A well-meaning employee who I imagined was reading from a well-thumbed script, told me I didn't need to be so upset because I still had 'memories' of my loved one to call on. Cloying, I know, but at the time it served as a necessary reminder that I wasn't the only person on the planet who had been bereaved.

I swam listlessly around the over-chlorinated pool, reflecting that my stay in the oasis had become cathartic in more ways than one: an outpouring of shit *and* grief. The self-help grief books hadn't helped. But what I was learning was that grief had to be respected. There was no point in pretending otherwise or trying to cheat it. If I felt like shit, I felt like shit. What was I expecting on this trip, a month-long *fiesta*?

When I climbed out of the pool I noticed a barefoot Quechua woman standing some ten metres away, with a huge bundle of laundry on her back. She called out to the girls. They gestured to her to come and meet me, but she remained motionless. As they all walked away, she looked back at me, smiled and waved. This simple gesture lifted my mood.

That evening, I heard what sounded like the clattering of hooves in the courtyard outside my room. I peered through the curtains. A television crew was busy rigging floodlights and setting up a huge table in preparation for what was about to become an exterior banqueting scene. A couple of dapple-grey thoroughbred horses were cantering around the courtyard, narrowly avoiding the continuity girls and make-up artists.

Ravishingly tanned women with ravine-like cleavages in flowery designer dresses and handsome, muscle-toned men in white cowboy hats slouched against the trees, lazily smoking. A Peruvian *Dallas*. I sat outside, listening to the Black Eyed Peas on my iPod, admiring these actors in their voluminous blonde wigs and tight-fitting jodhpurs.

Although my grief continued to throb away in the background, it didn't stop me appreciating the fresh morning air in the misty courtyard, Pedro the giant tortoise, or the warmth of the Mosonne staff. The longer I stayed, the friendlier they became. A waitress who was surly on day one, told me I'd become one of the family. I knew I had to eat but my appetite was minimal and the 'American breakfast' was becoming hard to swallow: *huevos, huevos, huevos* (eggs, eggs, eggs) every single morning. The recollection that *huevos* was also slang for 'bollocks' spurred me on to beg for something different. The kindly chef prepared me huge plates of *papaya*, my favourite fruit. *Caramba!*

# the witches' park

## who can I trust?

My stomach was on the mend and I was beginning to suffer from a bad dose of cabin fever. It was time to venture out of the oasis.

At Sacha's funeral reception I had overheard my father ask my writer friend, Vida, if she could get me writing again. Having a project, my dad believed, might distract his second daughter from her grief. Ten days later Vida asked if I would like to collaborate on a book about 21st-century witches and shamans.

I agreed to give it a go. In private, I felt as hugely ambivalent about her suggestion as I did about every other aspect of my existence. But I was sick of having to constantly reassure friends and family who were worried about me that I was, basically, OK. Maybe, if they thought I was suitably distracted, they might ease off a little.

Before I left England I promised my friend that I'd be on the lookout for a *bruja* or *chamán* to interview in Peru. And, according to my guide book, in the Ica region they were as plentiful as its vineyards.

Wine-tasting or witches? I certainly wouldn't have minded spending the day sampling the muscat-grape regional wine, but I didn't want to disappoint my friend. Besides, the little I'd read about these witches had actually managed to ignite in me something resembling a spark of curiosity for the first time in ages.

Spanish *brujas* fled to Peru in the 17th century to escape the Inquisition, only to be welcomed with outstretched arms by an even crueller Inquisition in Lima. Choosing to give Lima a miss, many headed for the Ica valley. Legend has it that the white witches settled in the Ica suburb of Cachiche, and the black witches in Huamangia.

No contest. It had to be Cachiche.

I waited a good twenty minutes in the taxi queue by the lagoon until, at last, a swarthy-looking driver with a droopy moustache and a huge gold medallion that clung, leech-like, to his chest guided me into his gleaming blue cab. His taxi was the newest and smartest I'd seen in Peru; already my suspicions were aroused. He reminded me of one of those archetypal Mexican *bandidos* who always popped up in 1970s cowboy movies.

I'd just about managed to convince myself, once we'd sped away, that my nervousness was simply post-Pan-American Highway paranoia, when he looked at me over his shoulder, grinned, and assured me I was safe with him because he was a police officer. With one hand on the steering wheel, he removed a wallet from his inside pocket and flashed his police ID card at me. It had *'retiro'* stamped across it in red letters.

He only looked about forty – way too young to be retired. Had he been 'retired' for a reason? Latin American cops have never had a particularly good reputation. Was I safe, I wondered, as we cruised past the monochrome suburbs of Ica. Should I jump out of this cab, too? Since learning what *really* went on at Sacha's prep school, I'd become hypervigilant around individuals who I suspected might have a malevolent agenda lurking behind their professional veneer. In short, I no longer knew whom I could trust and whom I couldn't.

My son's housemaster was in his late thirties, I guess. He was fat and ugly and wore glasses. That's the truth. His thinning hair curled up around his grubby collar. He had a bloated, red-veined boozer's face and his shirt stretched to its limits, so that the buttons could scarcely hold in his hairy, bulging belly. I couldn't bear him from the start.

The housemaster first attempted to become pally with me when he was directing Sacha in the musical *Bugsy Malone*. Sacha was Bugsy. Knowing I was a theatre writer and performer, the housemaster feigned a common interest and was cloyingly nice and ingratiating. He invited us both out for lunch a couple of times. I felt I had to accept, because to refuse could have been awkward for Sacha. I made the mistake of thinking he fancied me. I didn't know then that befriending a parent was all part of the grooming process.

A few months before his death, Sacha told me that, even as an adult, whenever he heard a snatch from the soundtrack of *Bugsy Malone* he would vomit.

The taxi pulled into Cachiche. I was surprised that, apart from a sparse-looking park and a few brightly painted houses, there was hardly anything or anyone there. Neither were there any vehicles, let alone taxis. I asked the driver to wait for me. Cachiche had gained popularity in the 1980s when a terminally ill politician was cured on national television by a shamanic healer, known in Peru as a *curandero*. The smallish suburb went on to become something of a spiritual tourist stop for alternative practitioners and pagans from around the world. I'd expected it to be packed.

A barefoot, unusually chubby Quechua boy of about ten waved and ran towards us. Panting away, the little lad knocked on my window and asked if I wanted him to tell me about the witches. I smiled, nodded and got out of the cab. He told us his name was Juan and then launched into an extremely lengthy gabble that he'd clearly learned off by heart, but didn't quite comprehend. Neither did I. His dialect was unfamiliar. The retired policeman-driver, who decided to get out the car too, didn't appear to understand much either.

Juan marched us over to a bronze statue of a young witch with outstretched arms which was attached to a *huarango* tree – the Peruvian 'tree of life' – and embarked on another virtually incomprehensible monologue. I could just about glean that the woman was Doña Julia, Cachiche's most famous witch, that the owl nestling beside her left foot represented wisdom, and the skull by her right, magic. Doña Julia had died twenty years earlier, Juan told us, at the age of 106.

Our young guide then took us around the flattened and deserted 'Witches' Park'. I was singularly unimpressed until he pointed out a gigantic palm tree with multiple splayed-out branches that should in theory have risen a good forty feet in the air but had instead grown horizontally adjacent to the ground. Juan claimed that, for centuries, witches had performed their ceremonies around this bizarre configuration. I stared at the earth-based tree and its alien-like mass of confused organic growth and then asked Juan if his mother was a witch. He shook his little head.

'*Mi madre no le gusta la magia.*'

I asked him why his mother didn't like magic. Rolling up the sleeve of his sweatshirt, he solemnly declared that his grandmother was a witch, and pointed to three horizontal faded white scars on his left forearm, each about an inch long. When he was seven she'd made the three cuts in his arm with a razor blade and rubbed silver onto them so that he would become rich.

In unconscious unison, the driver and I looked down at the boy's shoeless feet. The driver shook his head disapprovingly. Juan said his *mamá* was angry that his *abuela* had made him bleed. I sat down on a tree stump. I felt as queasy as I had when my son's English teacher told me at an open day that she'd seen cuts on Sacha's arms.

Sacha had reached puberty, and had moved on to a dyslexia-orientated boarding school near Winchester. I'd noticed a distinct change in him. His behaviour was bolshier and he exuded an indefinable sadness. When I asked him about the cuts, he made out that they were part of some macho penknife game-play he and his friends were into. I knew nothing then about self-harming and believed him, but on the advice of the concerned headmaster I took him to see a psychologist.

This bespoke 'professional', who was about sixty and claimed to be a devout Catholic, failed to identify that my son had been sexually abused. After a few sessions he said he reckoned Sacha was unhappy because he was much brighter than the other kids in his class and was de-motivated on account of it. When I explained that I was divorced from Sacha's father, the psychologist recommended I have a one-to-one session with him to explore how this could have affected Sacha. Towards the end of this session, he informed me that his ex-wife was evil, and that he found me very attractive. He said he'd like to have a relationship with me – that is, if I didn't smoke. I fled the consulting room, frightened and bewildered.

Although my parenting – and for that matter Roberto's lack of it – had been anything but perfect, Sacha had been a happy, carefree child who knew he was loved. I'd put his later moodiness and difficult behaviour down to the break-up of my second marriage to an American from North Carolina called Jake. We'd been together for several years and he and Sacha had become very close. Jake had happily and actively taken on the role of stepfather. Although he continued to see Sacha after the breakup, when he started working for American television networks in Beirut, at the time of the kidnapping of John McCarthy and other hostages, his visits to England became sporadic. In the end, Jake decided to return to the States. The breakup had deeply affected me, too.

Later in life, all I could relate Sacha's unhappiness and substance misuse to was a comment, on which he'd refused to elaborate, that he'd made in response to my probing: 'You shouldn't have sent me to boarding school, Mum.' I thought it was the familiar and understandable gripe that boarding school screws you up, until I trained as a psychotherapist.

I had made a decent living as a play/scriptwriter in the 1990s. But then, for one reason or another, seven projects I had in the pipeline got shelved and I realised I needed another string to my bow. I'd always been a good listener, and the complex internal universe we each inhabit fascinated me, so training as a therapist seemed like a good idea. It was also an opportunity to better understand and hopefully heal my own and my son's scarred psyches.

It was while attending a seminar as part of my training

at Sussex University, given by an expert on male abuse, that the grim possibility first dawned on me. The expert's behaviour profile of an abused male matched my son's: anger against authority; alcohol and substance misuse; low self-esteem; self-harm.

Up until that time, I'd been dismissive about the trauma that can ensue from sexual abuse. I'd even, as a writer, expressed cynicism at how frequently it was used in script plots as a *deus-ex-machina* device. And there I was, confronted with my own son's sordid reality. After the seminar I gently questioned Sacha, who was then in his early twenties. He ran out of the room. Eighteen months later, he confirmed that it was true.

I looked around the Witches' Park. Juan was busy wrapping a piece of chewing gum in a leaf. The driver was nowhere to be seen. He returned five minutes later and handed the boy an ice lolly.

The three of us hung out in the park taking cheesy photos of each other with my camera. It was fun, but I still wanted to know where all the witches were. My chirpy little guide led me to the house of 'the best' *chamán* in town, whose showy neon sign read: '*Salud, Dinero y Amor*', and advised me that as well as delivering health, money and love, this *chamán* could also predict the future. I was about to knock on the door when I suddenly developed cold feet: the last 'future' reading I'd had – at a psychic fair in Earl's Court in the 1980s with a self-proclaimed witch – had really spooked me out.

The reading had taken place around the time that Jake and I were going to get married – mainly because he needed a visa to stay in the country. The witch was adamant that the marriage wouldn't work out. She went on to tell me I'd meet a guy who I'd be really happy with for ten years – then he'd die. Forcing a wicker doll on me, she insisted I'd need it for protection. I went ahead with the marriage anyway, but as it transpired, she was right about the marriage not working out. Jake and I separated six months later. When I met David, I felt considerable angst that this was the second guy she'd been referring to. I now realise the 'he' was Sacha, who died in the tenth year of my marriage to David.

Since that encounter, I'd become witch-wary, at least where predicting the future was concerned; clairvoyant consultations achieved very little, apart from either filling the punter with dread or making them overly passive. And did I really want to fork out money to interview someone whose dialect I might also have difficulty understanding? Besides, I'd already interviewed one shaman that year, and he'd had a lot more to offer than 'health, money and love'.

This shaman, who had come highly recommended, was essentially a healer and lived in Worthing, of all places, with his mousy wife. I was curious to see if he could help me cope with my grief, as bereavement counselling was doing zilch for me at the time. I also wanted an interview for the book.

The Worthing shaman was a tall, craggy, once-handsome guy in his mid-fifties, with a ley-lined face and a double-barrelled name, who claimed to be the illegitimate son of a Scottish lord. A self-confessed lone wolf, he was an off-the-radar oddball. Some would call him a fantasist, others downright bonkers, but I was in no doubt that his power was real.

It came, he claimed, from the universe. He told me he was in contact with beings from other planets who understood the secret of immortality. He pointed out a globe in the waiting room with gold stars on it, depicting spaceship stop-off points. Certain evolved people, he assured me, could attain eternal life through extensive healing on a cellular level. I, apparently, was one of them.

Unsurprisingly, at that time the prospect of eternal life held absolutely no joy for me. In fact, the very thought of it was positively hellish. That aside, the night after seeing the shaman for the first time, I had a wonderful dream about Sacha. It felt so real. No. More than real – it felt like it was actually happening. In it, Sacha was around ten years old. We were flying together at tremendous, exhilarating speed above Nordic pine forests, Niagara-like waterfalls and sky-rise cities. As the dream drew to a close we had a wonderful, long hug. I awoke, exhilarated.

After that, I saw the shaman fortnightly for a couple of months and managed to interview him in the process. The sessions certainly took the edge off my suffering and also lifted some of the negative energy I was inevitably picking up from the clients I counselled. I always drove home feeling relaxed and peaceful. A couple of friends and my sister Sally also felt the beneficial power of his energy. He diagnosed a health issue by looking at Sally's eyes in a photograph she'd emailed him, and sent her remote healing. When she finally saw him in person, she was so spaced out after the session that she walked straight into a lamppost.

After a time, there was no hiding the fact that the shaman had a crush on me. I was initially flattered. It isn't every day a girl gets the offer of immortality, having her enemies crushed, and being told she can jump onto a spaceship 'the size of Portsmouth' and be ferried around the universe. When you're in the thick of grief you're desperate for any kind of distraction.

I'd lie on his couch, wondering what planet I was on. My ungrounded head-state wasn't helped by the fact that, staring down at me from a Hollywood film poster on the consulting-room wall, was a young actor I was counselling at the time. He and Sacha were the same age, of similar appearance and had a great deal in common, including a love of dogs and an unhappy childhood. Yet the actor had reached the heights and Sacha the depths. Never mind life on other planets, I remember thinking; the disparate realities inhabited by these two young men were alien enough for me.

Our sessions came to a pretty abrupt end. One afternoon, the shaman informed me that his autobiography was proving to be a huge hit with young Goths in Eastern Europe who were into vampires and immortality, and then asked me if

I'd like to live with him in Greece. I doubted his wife or my husband would have been too keen on the idea and, for that matter, neither was I. As I left his room for the last time, I couldn't resist asking him why he himself didn't visit other planets. He replied that he wasn't evolved enough.

Death takes you to some intriguing places.

The retired policeman-taxi driver was mooching disconcertedly around the witches' den. It was time to go. I gave Juan a good tip and, for the first time, his serious little face beamed up at me. When he dropped me off at La Plaza des Armas in Ica, my retired policeman-taxi driver was also happy with his tip. I'd warmed to him. Slowly. It was the ice lolly that melted me.

My recent dealings with the English police had left me feeling warmer towards them, too. Katie, a young woman sergeant in Brighton assigned to investigate Sacha's death, came to interview me at home. It lasted for a gruelling three hours. Katie was an empathic young woman who appeared to connect with Sacha's life. She was the same age, and was also dyslexic.

My son had developed an immense dislike for the police and all they stood for after he was arrested in Holland Park at the age of fifteen. Several police had been roughing up a black guy and Sacha, typically, went to his aid. In the scuffle that ensued, both Sacha and a policeman got their noses broken. The son of a high-ranking police officer and his girlfriend were in the park at the time and saw it all. They went immediately to Holland Park police station to make a complaint about police brutality.

I bumped into this pair when I was collecting Sacha, and they offered themselves as witnesses. But although they gave evidence in court, the officers lied about what had happened, and Sacha's key witness, a nervous young friend who had been with him at the time, went to pieces in the dock. After months of nerve-wracking adjournments and reports, Sacha was given a fine and a suspended sentence.

At the end of the statement I made for Katie, I expressed my concern that the paedophile housemaster could still be around, ruining the lives of other kids.

Once Sacha finally told me about the sexual abuse, three years before his death, I hoped we might be able to bring the man to justice. But Sacha would say, 'He's dead, Mum, he's dead,' whenever I mentioned the housemaster, in a tone that meant the conversation and prospect of taking it any further was finished. Over. Dead.

A week after Sacha's funeral, my sister Suzanne and I trawled through all the letters my son had written to me from his prep school, and also those I'd written to him, to try to find the paedophile's name. Eventually, we found it and I was able to pass it on to Katie, along with the annual school photographs which included the man in question.

Katie set to work with a vengeance. If the man were

found, there would be no possibility of bringing him to trial, as Sacha wasn't alive to give evidence, but she was worried about other kids too, and wanted the housemaster to know the police were on to him. She also thought he should know what suffering he'd caused to Sacha and his family and friends.

Her task wasn't an easy one. The prep school had since closed, and the local education authority held no records. She managed to trace the elderly, retired headmaster and went to interview him in his home. She told me he remembered Sacha fondly and was visibly upset when he heard the sad history of his former pupil. But he didn't know what had become of the school records or the housemaster, whom he had sacked for throwing a boy against the wall and injuring him. He also didn't have that most essential piece of information, the paedophile's date of birth, which made tracing him very difficult. Katie tried every possible avenue, but without a date of birth her search was futile. She even brought in an expert 'tracer' but, because there were no leads, he had no success. I remember thinking, at the time, that perhaps Sacha was right; the paedophile was, indeed, dead.

Katie stayed in touch. When she was moved from crime to security, she rang me to tell me she was taking Sacha's file with her. He had touched her life as he'd touched the lives of many others. How I wish Sacha could have met her.

Ten years later, when an earlier version of this book came out, I was contacted by several former students of the prep school and also by family members of children who had attended it at the same time as my son. They had read articles in the national press about Sacha and the abuse he'd endured there. It became apparent that the abuse wasn't limited to that one teacher. I heard sad tales of addiction, mental illness and even the imprisonment for anti-social behaviour of some of Sacha's contemporaries. Eventually one former member of staff was sent to prison for seven years for abusing two brothers at the school. The police also managed, finally, to trace Sacha's abuser, who, it transpired, was living in the South West. Disappointingly, no one was prepared to give evidence against him, so he couldn't be charged. One former student told me he felt too ashamed to stand up in court and admit that he'd been sexually abused. What did give me some reassurance was that the police alerted schools and children's services in the area to the paedophile's presence in their vicinity.

Feeling hungry for the first time in days, I dived into the nearest restaurant, just off Ica's La Plaza des Armas, and ordered a plate of chicken *empanadas*. I was the only customer in the restaurant – and I soon realised why.

The moment my food arrived a middle-aged 'musician' appeared from nowhere, positioned himself beside my table and placed a chipped ceramic bowl with some coins in it next to my bottle of *Cusqueña* beer. He was wearing all the right gear: a dazzling patterned poncho and felt *sombrero* over his heavily-beaded *chullo*, and his ukulele-like instrument – which was, he explained, a ten-stringed *charango* made from the shell of an armadillo – looked the business too. But for the life of him he couldn't play it or manage to hit a single note when he sang.

I suspected that the bulging *chuspa* around his waist wasn't stuffed full of the coca leaves that it's designed to carry, but cash that customers like myself had foisted upon him in the hope that he'd piss off and let them eat their meal in peace. I chanced it and placed a substantial number of coins in his bowl. But my generosity didn't have the desired effect and he serenaded me with additional vigour. The waitress caught my eye. Hers were twinkling. We both suppressed a giggle.

To distract myself, I switched on my phone and sent an upbeat text to David. I didn't want to take him or my 'third-time-lucky' marriage for granted. His German-Jewish mother had come to England as a *kindertransport* refugee and had subsequently lost her parents in the Holocaust. He'd grown up in the shadow of her survivor's-guilt misery. The last thing he needed was a partner with it, too.

David's response was swift: he was on his way to visit his (English) father and Flemish stepmother at their smallholding in a remote part of Belgium. He said it was dark and snowing heavily; the roads were icy and dangerous.

The heat in the restaurant was blistering. I looked through the window at the dazzling Inca sun and reflected, for a few moments, on our diverse realities; then, giving up on the *empanadas*, I paid and left.

Once outside, I noticed for the first time that the name of restaurant was *Las Brujas de Cachiche*.

# crystals and crusties

## extreme highs

Huacachina lagoon exuded a magical, otherworldly aura at night. Myth has it that the lagoon was formed when a naked princess, about to perform her ablutions, saw the reflection of an admiring hunter in her mirror. She dropped the mirror, which smashed into thousands of fragments and metamorphosed into a glistening expanse of water.

Late one night, I slipped out to buy a bottle of water and noticed some unusual reflections on the surface of the lagoon. A hippy-looking woman of Hispanic descent had set up a stall on the bank and was selling huge quartz crystals. She told me the crystals were from the Peruvian Andes. Glittering in the moonlight, they were some of the finest I'd ever seen. I've been collecting crystals, on and off, for years. I had to have one, but first I needed to change some more money. I promised to return the following evening.

Back at the Mosonne I was disconcerted to discover that three English guys were busy moving into the rooms adjoining mine. Now I'd have to share the tranquil courtyard that I'd had more or less to myself all week. There was a great deal of door-slamming, beery laughter and general commotion. Pedro had receded into his shell. I scuttled into my room, unseen.

The next morning as I was on my way out of the hotel to visit the Ica museum, one of my new neighbours looked up from his *Financial Times* and started to chat. I pulled up a chair and sat beside him on the terrace.

His two travelling companions had hired a dune buggy to go sandboarding, he told me, but he'd broken his ankle snowboarding in Canada the previous year and didn't want to risk breaking it again. He was also feeling nauseous after some early-morning aerial sightseeing in a private plane they'd hired in Ica.

It was his first time in South America. The three of them were, he explained, bankers working in the City of London, who were 'doing Peru' in two weeks.

'We're in a rush,' he said, 'because we're money-rich and time-poor.'

'I'm money-poor and time-rich,' I responded, 'and I hope, very soon, to try some low-key sandboarding myself.'

How was it possible, I privately wondered, to 'do' a country? My experience of travel was that a country 'did' me: unfamiliar vistas and experiences – some welcome, others less so – unleashed hidden realms in my heart and soul. For Sacha, it was like that too. My new neighbour made travel sound more like a box-ticking exercise.

The banker's name was Simon, and he seemed pleasant enough. He must have been around Sacha's age and was clearly ex-public school, but then my son was a public schoolboy too, until he became one of the very few pupils to be expelled from his establishment. (Madonna's ex-husband Guy Ritchie, who attended the same school a few years earlier, was another.)

Sacha's expulsion, for being caught with a Swiss army knife on a school outing, actually came as something of a relief. We'd both had enough of him boarding and I was about to put our London flat in Earl's Court on the market and move closer to Winchester so that he could become a day-boy. I gave up house hunting and registered fourteen-year-old Sacha at Holland Park Comprehensive, up the road.

I couldn't help wondering what Sacha would have made of my banker neighbours. He could be quite judgemental about people with lots of dosh. I very much doubted that Simon and his friends were into the post-rave, free party, techno scene – an amalgam of warehouse partygoers from various urban-squat scenes and politically inspired New Age Travellers – that Sacha had been part of.

When he first visited South America as an independent traveller with his Australian girlfriend Angie, Sacha didn't stay in the Lima Sheraton like Simon and his friends; he slept mainly in a tent and even spent some time in a jail cell in Ecuador.

After visiting relatives in Bogotá, Sacha and Angie had intended to head for Peru, but the day before they were due to leave, a coach-load of tourists were killed by guerrillas on the Colombian/Bolivian border, so they decided to stay put. Shortly afterwards, following a huge row, Angie flew back to England on the spur of the moment. As soon as the plane touched down, she deeply regretted it. So did I; it marked the beginning of my Sacha travel nightmares.

Although his belongings were still in a hostel in Bogotá, neither Angie nor I could get hold of him – nor could his Colombian relatives. I spent a hellish few weeks waiting for news until, eventually, Sacha called me from Ecuador.

Sounding shaky and emotional, he said he'd just been let out of jail. Corrupt police had arrested him after questioning his signature on his traveller's cheques, and then demanded a bribe – amounting to just about all of his remaining money – to release him. Fortunately, relatives of the prisoner in the adjoining cell had brought him food. He'd held out for two weeks but eventually couldn't stand it any more and paid up. Angry and relieved, I sent money over via American Express and he came straight home.

Sacha and Angie were reconciled upon his return – but only briefly. Angie was lovely, but it was a tempestuous relationship that never got back on its feet after their big bust-up. She wanted to settle down, but Sacha still wanted to travel. Angie's parents were wealthy business people and her father offered Sacha a good job in his company if he went to Australia, but Sacha declined. We all thought he was mad at the time. Angie's visa ran out and she had to leave without him.


In Ica's celebrated Museo Regional, I stared in wonder at the strange Nazca mummies curled up in foetal positions in glass cases, with food and artefacts for the afterlife at their feet. Some had the most amazingly huge trepanned skulls. The *cabeza larga* (long head), as it's known, was formed by wrapping the heads of newborn babies with leather or wood, causing their skulls to grow into extraordinary shapes. This deformation gave them the appearance of comic-book intergalactic aliens, in keeping with some of the wilder theories concerning the origins of the famous Nazca Lines which lie a couple of hours' drive south of Ica.

The Nazca formed these lines over hundreds of years. There doesn't appear to be a consensus on the timeline but they were arguably designed between 200 BC and 600 AD. They were made by carving through the bush and stones of the plain to expose the lighter, dusty soil underneath, and then piling stones on either side. The mystery surrounding them is that they're virtually imperceptible at ground level. These Lines – and the designs and shapes the Nazca also carved into the landscape – can only be properly discerned from the sky. The writer Erich von Däniken was convinced the Lines were extraterrestrial landing sites made by aliens from outer space.

One of the mummies, encased in glass, had hair – or rather dreads – of a dark-brown colour down to its ankles. I 'hear' Sacha laughing. His dreads were the same rich colour and he was proud of them, although they only reached as far as his shoulder blades.

I recalled an old picture from *The Times* that a friend of Sacha's handed me at his funeral: Sacha at Glastonbury, knee-deep in mud in the pouring rain, his dreads flying around in the wind, laughing with a couple of friends. I wondered what drugs they were on.

Along with quite a few, mainly middle-class, kids of his generation, Sacha became involved in the New Age Traveller scene. Encouraged by bands such as the Levellers, they liked to hit the road. Rejecting consumerist society and promoting environmentalism, sustainability and mutual aid, New Age Travellers were the hippies of the 1990s, only better organised. They also liked their drugs.

In the mid-1990s, I was commissioned by a magazine to write an article about these people. My research proved to be something of an eye-opener. Society and the media often confused them with the traditional travellers and with the notorious 'Brew Crew' – homeless social outsiders and ex-convicts who consumed vast amounts of Special Brew.

But New Agers had very strict codes of behaviour, one of them being that they would always leave a site cleaner than they found it. Bob Dylan had advised an earlier generation that if they wanted to live outside the law they had to be honest, and most New Agers adhered to this. I was impressed with some – but not all – of the Travellers I met, and quite shocked by the level of harassment they received from the police.

The zenith of the free party scene was the Castlemorton Common Festival where, with less than 24 hours' notice and very little publicity, more than 35,000 had gathered for five days of partying. The response to the outrage this provoked in Middle England was the passing, in 1994, of the Criminal Justice and Public Order Act which, slowly but effectively, killed off the free party scene in England. Travellers were left with little choice but to move abroad with their sound systems. Sacha found well-paid work rigging sound systems in Europe.

In the courtyard outside the Museo Regional, a lone alpaca was grazing on weeds. I sat myself on a bench and started reading up on the Nazca people. It appeared that they, too, liked their drugs. 'Teacher plants', such as the mescaline cactus San Pedro, which is still used by Peruvian shamans today, helped to induce the Nazca's out-of-body shamanic flights. I looked up as a grey raptor swooped graciously beneath the mackerel sky. Back inside the museum I paid five sol to take a photograph of the mummy with the spectacular dreads.

When we were clearing out Sacha's flat after his death I found his beloved dreads under the stairs in a plastic carrier bag. Thinking it would be too painful to hold on to, I threw out the tangled, cocoa-coloured mane – and later regretted it. The dreads had eventually been lopped off, at Sacha's request, in the back of a truck in Bulgaria, by a girl who was part of the free party sound crew he was working with at the time.

Simon was still sitting on the terrace when I got back to the hotel. He'd shaved his prematurely balding head and was vigorously rubbing sun-cream into it. He looked anxious: his friends hadn't yet returned from their sandboarding expedition and they were scheduled to leave for Arequipa in two hours' time.

He invited me for a beer, and we headed for the terrace bar overlooking the lagoon. When he wasn't trying to catch glimpses of his friends in the dunes through his binoculars, we talked about the stresses of travelling, Starbucks, insider trading and coke snorting in the City.

I told him about two clients of mine who were both City bankers and heavy coke users. One was a woman counting down the biological clock and in the process of purchasing a *château* in France; she was so stressed, her hair was starting to fall out. The other was a forty-something guy who wanted to give it all up and become a potter, but didn't think his marriage would survive without his annual bonus.

Chuckling, Simon said that in the late 1990s he used to fly to New York for weekend coke parties on the Lower East Side, hosted by a glamorous transsexual Colombian dealer. My son was in Colombia at around the same time, snorting bag-loads of that white powder, too.

Sacha's initial reason for going to Colombia was to help his father restore a large old Spanish colonial house in Santa Marta – the Colombian equivalent of a listed building that Roberto had recently bought. He took with him his best friend Phil, a sculptor; Piran, an old mate from school who was a carpenter; and Emma, an attractive, warm-hearted blonde, also part of the Traveller scene.

But as it panned out, Roberto was endlessly delayed at work, leaving the four of them to camp out and fend for themselves in this virtual ruin. Sacha was a serial moaner at the best of times, and this unappealing trait was amplified by the situation the friends now found themselves in. Phil teased him endlessly about his moaning.

This was another dangerous time to be in South America: El Niño; mudslides in Peru; fires in Brazil; elections in Colombia; and the frequent kidnapping of foreigners. Sacha had wanted to take his friends to Machu Picchu, but it wasn't safe.

Emma and Phil found travelling with Sacha great fun at times because he knew the places to go and all the good beaches, but it could also be scary. Why? Cocaine was very cheap and very plentiful.

Phil, who knew nothing about Sacha's troubled history until after his death, was becoming increasingly concerned about his friend's drug-taking. He told me he'd hoped, in Colombia, to be able to thrash out with Sacha the reason for his high drug usage. But Sacha, apparently, was coked up for so much of the time that the opportunity never presented itself.

Matters came to a head when, according to Sacha, a Colombian guy he'd just met slipped something into his drink in a bar in Santa Marta. The guy then invited him back to his place, with, Sacha believed, the intention of robbing him. Realising his drink had been spiked, Sacha somehow managed to stagger back to the house and proceeded to have a serious psychotic episode. His friends had to take him to hospital, where he ended up in a psychiatric unit.

A fellow Traveller and friend with a PhD in pharmaceuticals intervened. He figured out that the drink had been spiked with the 'date rape' drug Rohypnol. Thanks to his efforts, Sacha was released from hospital. Distraught, he rang and asked me to send him, once again, the money to fly home as soon as possible.

His travel traumas were beginning to take on a familiar pattern. He loved South America, but it was a dangerous place for someone of Sacha's temperament and inclinations.

The following year, Roberto abandoned the restoration of the house in Santa Marta and sold it for a pittance. Cartels and kidnappings made it just too dangerous to stay in the area, even for him, a Colombian national.

Just as I was wondering whether I'd have preferred Sacha to be an investment banker like Simon rather than a New Age Traveller – and weighing up the sometimes dubious ethics that underpinned both – Simon's banker friends returned from their sandboarding adventure. The stockier of the two had come off his board and injured his upper arm; it was bleeding quite heavily. They both traipsed off to get him bandaged up.

Dispirited, Simon ordered another beer and told me how he'd suffered burnout after his New York weekends. Fearful of losing his head and getting into speculative rogue trading like Nick Leeson, he'd replaced his coke highs with skydiving in Kuala Lumpur and skeet shooting in Wyoming (as you do).

Once, for a dare, Sacha leaped off the twenty-metre high Mostar Bridge in Bosnia, famed for its annual daredevil 'jumping off' competition – clutching, he told me, his balls. He was working in Eastern Europe, sound rigging for a DJ and his sound system called Dubious. Sacha and the crew had many scary adventures – including being shot at by drunken Bulgarian soldiers – of which he seemed bizarrely proud.

When he wasn't on the road, Sacha lived, like many Travellers, in urban squats, and breaking into them was something at which he became adept. He believed that leaving property empty when thousands of people were homeless was immoral. When the eviction notices were served, which was about every six months, they moved into a different squat. Phil and Sacha's 'ethical' squatting gave me many a sleepless night.

Simon's banker friend returned with his arm in a sling and a bag full of painkillers. Sadly, his accident put paid to any sandboarding ambitions I'd harboured. What these bankers and Sacha actually did have in common, I realised, apart from liberal drug use, was a love of extreme sports – which I certainly didn't share.

That evening, I returned to the lagoon-side stall and took my time choosing a crystal. We haggled politely for a couple of minutes and finally agreed on 25 sol for a jagged, translucent crystal about the size of a Galia melon. My crystal lady instructed me to 'cleanse' the crystal every now and then by placing it in a shaft of moonlight when the moon was full. Quartz crystals, she told me, were still an important part of shamanic ceremonies in Peru and in Colombia; the Desana peoples viewed them as a crystallisation of solar energy and a means of communication between the visible and invisible realms.

As she carefully wrapped my purchase in reams of newspaper, I told her that crystals were in our genes. She looked at me quizzically. I explained that the Austrian physicist and father of quantum mechanics, Erwin Schrödinger, who had a life-long interest in Hindu Vedanta philosophy, floated the idea in the 1940s that the chromosome was an 'aperiodic crystal'. His intuition led, a decade later, to the discovery of DNA.

What I didn't tell her was that when I thought of crystals, I also thought of Rebecca who, for a week before Sacha's funeral, wore a crystal in her bra before placing it in his coffin.

Sacha and Rebecca were together for almost seven years, although the last sixteen months they spent apart. With her long black hair, pale skin, huge brown eyes and figure to die for, Rebecca was a beautiful woman who knew how to fix the engines of trucks, and for many years drove her own truck around Europe. Delightfully dippy, sometimes maddeningly so, she was enterprising and energetic, with a great sense of fun.

They met on a settee on Toulouse Plage, a riverside beach in the French city, a sound system blaring out behind them. It was, according to both of them, love at first sight. Rebecca was travelling with a sound system called Hecate, which pitched up at a festival in Toulouse at the same time as the Dubious system Sacha was working with. They went to a few bars in town, then headed for the coast, where they wandered off into the sand dunes and made love under the stars.

Sacha called me the next day to say that he'd fallen in love, really in love, for the first time. Phil remembers him returning from a rigging tour of France with a photograph of a woman called Rebecca, and telling him with a grin: 'She even likes my moaning'.

Two nights before I left for Peru, Rebecca appeared on my doorstep, after a three-hour drive, and presented me with an exquisitely embroidered orange silk pouch she'd sewn for the transportation of Sacha's ashes. She also made me promise to email her from my trip.

I left the crystal stall and made my way to the internet café, where there was an email waiting for me from Rebecca: 'I know Sacha's happy, I just know… More than ever in the last year, the whole way you are doing this, going to Machu Picchu for him, is so…right. By the way, I didn't want to say when I delivered the orange pouch for the ashes, but I sewed some of my hair into the lining, just so's I could be with him… I feel you and Sacha so strongly at the moment. I'm with you every step of the way.'

The moon was full and the stars ice-clear. I sipped vegetable soup on the veranda of a lagoon-side restaurant, and marvelled at the alchemical reflection in the mirror of the motionless water – as above, so below.

A large white lorry pulled up, obscuring my view of the lagoon. The driver was delivering crates of fruit and vegetables to the restaurant. My eyes welled up, as I remembered the much newer, bigger and whiter lorry that Sacha and Rebecca had bought and converted into a comfortable home for themselves.

A few months earlier they'd set up a company called Headflux which designed, printed and sold hoodies and T-shirts. The designs caught on and before long they were getting plenty of orders from festivals and shops in both England and Europe. They set off in their white lorry/home for Europe and continued marketing their wares at shops and festivals on the continent.

They also shared a sound system called Sound Conspiracy with Emma and her partner, which had its own speakers, music, backdrops and decorations. The four friends had a strong bond and often travelled together in France, Austria and the Czech Republic. At festivals and weekend-long 'free parties' they provided a bar and food and took donations on the door from Travellers and locals.

Emma described their life on the road as a kind of communal living, which included all the highs and lows that went with it. One week they'd make good money and be able to afford decent food and wine. The following week they'd make nothing and live on scraps.

David and I met Sacha and Rebecca for a few lovely days in Argelès-sur-Mer in the south of France. I'd rarely seen Sacha so happy. Headflux and Sound Conspiracy were doing well and his finances had increased along with his confidence. Sacha told us they had a plan to take their lorry full of toys to sick, malnourished children in the devastated region of Chernobyl. He clearly had the arrival movie playing in his head when, with animated eyes, he said, 'Just imagine their little faces lighting up, Mum, when we open the truck and all these toys come pouring out. Can't you just picture it?'

I certainly could picture it, only too well, but it wasn't to happen.

After the usual polite 'where are you from?' enquiries, the chatty waiter came out with the now-familiar dreaded question: how many children did I have? I paused, then replied, 'None.' The temptation to tell him I had a son who was alive and happy in the UK or South America or wherever, not in an orange silk pouch in the safe of my hotel room thirty metres away, was suddenly overwhelming. But I knew I couldn't go there.

To reassure me that I hadn't missed out too much on the whole propagation experience, the kindly waiter took away my soup bowl, plonked my pasta dish on the table, then sat down and shared all the trials and tribulations he was having with his own kids and their school in Ica.

As I listened to his monologue I gazed up at the sky. I hadn't seen such an immaculate full moon since the week before Sacha's death. I had called him to the kitchen window because that last December moon, like this one, resembled a gigantic pumpkin, suspended so low in the sky you could almost touch it. We stood together for a long time, lost in lunar admiration.

I made my way back to the hotel, returning the smiles and waves of a stall-keeper's kids who were still splashing around in the moonlit lagoon.

Rebecca told me that, as an antidote to grief, she played her flute, hammering and blasting out notes to achieve an emotional release. The Waterboys' song 'The Whole Of The Moon' from their album *The Sea* had really churned her up since Sacha's death. I asked her why it resonated so strongly for her. Her lovely brown eyes welled up. Giving me a sad 'don't you get it?' look she said, 'I saw the crescent, Diane, but Sacha saw the whole of the moon.'

I was devastated to discover, when I climbed out of bed the following morning, that my gorgeous Andean crystal had, fallen onto the parquet floor during the night and smashed into three fragments. I realised that in my sleep I must have knocked it off the adjoining bed. I was annoyed with myself for unwrapping it in the first place. As I picked up the stalactite-like shards, cutting my finger in the process, I thought about the naked princess's shattered mirror that had created the lagoon. I was very upset, but I couldn't help feeling the crystal had split for a reason.

That evening, my last in Huacachina, I decided I was finally strong enough to head for the monster dune in the distance that had been tantalising me all week. If I managed to scale it, I would be able to watch the sun sink over the vast desert beyond. The climb was arduous, and the sand slippery in places. When I eventually reached the dune top, I gazed out onto a deathly still moonscape wilderness; an infinity of yellow, devoid of sound or life. Was this what death is like, I wondered.

Exhilarated but weak, I pushed myself to climb a further dune to get a little closer to the flamingo sky. Once there, I sat down on the warm sand to get my breath back. Then, sensing Sacha beside me, I chanted quietly until Sacha 'whispered' to me – 'Better get going, Mum' – and he was right. As the sun slipped below the dune horizon, it suddenly grew unnervingly dark. I slid down the giant dune on my bum, loving every minute of it.

Back in my room, I celebrated my magical safari, renewed strength and improved mood by drinking a cocktail of peach juice and *uvachado* – a sort of grape liqueur I'd bought in Lima, but hadn't had the stomach to try until then. It tasted sublime.

Before going to bed I removed the ashes from the safe and carefully re-wrapped the shards of crystal. It dawned on me that my big Andean crystal had smashed because it wanted to be shared. One fragment was for me. One fragment was for Phil. One fragment was for Rebecca.

# the skeleton families

## heroin hell

The interior of the hour-late Royal double-decker coach taking me from Ica to Nazca the next day reminded me of a 1990s charter plane which had seen better days; its reclining seats were threadbare, its windows sand-stained.

As I settled into my window seat on the upper floor I spotted the bus station hero who had rescued my suitcase from the Bolivia-bound coach the week before, and who was heaving the suitcase back on board. I waved frantically as the coach pulled away. It took a few moments for him to recognise me, then he waved back.

Half an hour into the journey, a uniformed Royal hostess emerged from behind a curtain and meandered up and down the coach, offering meals of bluish-looking slush and orange squash in plastic cups. Having taken the last of my diarrhoea tablets that morning, I declined the meal but accepted the drink.

As I sipped my squash I gazed out of the window, mesmerised by the wild scenery on a strip of desert known as the Pampa de Gamonal. Besides having one of the most varied climates on the planet, Peru also has deep canyons, high mountains, active volcanoes, glaciers, equatorial dry forests, Amazon jungle and the driest desert on earth.

The Pampa de Gamonal was named after a local chief who stashed all his treasure in this section of the desert, but couldn't relocate it once a fierce sand storm had remodelled the landscape. It must have driven him crazy. Frequented by ferocious gale-force winds, the sculptured, ash-like dunes and contorted rock formations in this barren land appeared to cling vicariously to the fickle desert sands. I was beginning to lose myself in the sheer 'otherness' of Peru.

After a couple of hours, the small, sprawling colonial town of Nazca, peppered with squatter camps, gradually came into view. The river was dry, but the coastal valley along which the town was built had remained fertile thanks to the Incas who, hundreds of years ago, were savvy enough to build a subterranean aqueduct there.

The coach pulled into what resembled a large prison yard – only the 'prisoners' were leaning on the outside of the tall metal grids that surrounded the yard, staring in. The driver announced that we'd arrived at Nazca bus station and an unsettling thought occurred to me: perhaps these fortifications had been put in place to keep out the touts.

A couple of us disembarked and, sure enough, around thirty touts moved towards the barred exit gate and pressed themselves up behind it. A bus station employee helped the driver unload our luggage, then, hesitantly, unlocked the gate.

The touts made a beeline for me, as I was the only Gringo leaving the sanctuary of the bus station. They swarmed around, screeching: 'Hotel?... Taxi?... Restaurant?... Tour?... Nazca Lines?' Half a dozen or so of them tried to grab my suitcase. Clutching onto the rucksack containing the ashes and my valuables, I shoved my way through the crowd. Dragging my case behind me, I followed a guy – who said he was a taxi driver – to his car.

Just as he was about to close the boot with my suitcase inside, a woman with a clipboard ran over and started screaming at him that he was unlicensed. She pulled my case out of the boot and insisted that it was dangerous for me to go with him. Another woman started yelling at her that she was lying. A fight nearly broke out. Then someone shouted, 'Tourist police!' and the crowd dispersed. I asked the woman with the clipboard to find me a licensed cab, which she eventually did.

The taxi dropped me off at the Montecarlo Hotel, where I'd made a reservation a couple of nights earlier. A sweet old man escorted me to a dilapidated chalet room bordering a 'swimming pool', which had an interesting array of multicoloured plastic bottles bobbing up and down in its six inches of shit-coloured water.

How out of date some of these 'up-to-the-minute latest-edition' travel guides are! This 'interesting and rambling hotel with a swimming pool' didn't match up to its guidebook description, nor had it done so, I guessed, for quite some time. I'd opted for the Montecarlo because, according to the guide, the owners did their own flights over the Nazca Lines. Ye gods! If the state of their pool was anything to go by, I wondered who in their right mind would want to put a foot inside their aeroplane.

I shook my head apologetically, tipped the old boy and asked him to call a licensed taxi. He nodded, and gave me an understanding smile. I waited in the deserted lobby wondering what delights Nazca might offer up next. I didn't have to wait long. The taxi that he summoned arrived with its very own tout. Seated next to the driver and dressed in a bright floral shirt and leather trousers, a podgy-looking guy with Elvis hair and a two-day stubble leaned over and introduced himself as César.

César recommended a hotel on the edge of town called the Don Agucho. As I hadn't a clue where else to go, I agreed to take a look.

Adorned with huge, colourful, flowering cacti, the Don Agucho had the appearance and the vibe of a hospitable *hacienda*; relieved, I paid upfront for two nights. César collected his tip from the hotel owners and offered to book me a flight over the Nazca Lines for no small sum. I told him I'd think about it. Only after I'd unpacked my suitcase and hung my clothes in the naphthalene-smelling wardrobe did I discover that the Don Agucho wasn't as hospitable as I'd hoped. The restaurant was closed, the dour manageress informed me, due to a shortage of guests. I was left with the grim choice of walking the fair distance into Nazca town and facing yet more touts, or going hungry.

Annoyed that I'd succumbed to such negative thinking where touts were concerned, I ordered myself to get over it and go into town. Given the choice, and of course the money, I'm sure these people would rather have been astrophysicists or cosmetic surgeons. But they happened to be living in a small town with the Nazca Lines as the only major tourist attraction, in a very poor country when the tourist season hadn't yet kicked off. Even if they weren't land squatters, they still had rent to pay and families to feed. I was grateful I'd never had to live in the shadow of such poverty.

How easily I slipped into being judgemental, I chastised myself, as I slathered on anti-mosquito cream in preparation for my outing – and I was the mother of a junkie who got riled when she heard anyone being judgemental about *them*. Just as most chronic drug use is caused by chronic pain and no one actually *chooses* to be an addict, very few of those people outside the bus station, I reminded myself, had actually chosen to be touts.

I meandered into the mosquito-infested centre of Nazca in the hope of finding an inviting restaurant. Nothing grabbed me, so I bought a few edible supplies from a run-down mini-market and consumed them outside an Italian archaeological museum.

The museum itself housed an inferior version of what was on display at Ica's museum. The main items of interest were the three ginger kittens with whom I played in the foyer and a lively young girl in school uniform who sold me a drink from her stall at the entrance. She told me she worked there in the evenings and at weekends to give her mother a break, but would rather be at home doing her homework.

This was the first time a child had ever said to me they'd rather be doing their homework, and I told her so. She looked surprised. Children who went to school, like her, were very privileged, she said. I wished I'd had this encounter when I was a lazy, grumbling schoolkid.

Over the years, travelling in countries poorer than my own has opened my eyes to many aspects of my life that I'd simply taken for granted. Spending time in drought-ridden Africa helped me to appreciate the water flowing out of my taps back home. I remember once watching an item on local television news about the effects of a hosepipe ban in southern England. I'd recently returned from Nigeria where I'd seen women and children trudging miles to wells every day to collect water. A well-to-do woman was being interviewed in her leafy garden. She was in tears because the ban meant she had to switch her sprinklers off and use a watering can. I yearned to whisk her away to see a truly drought-ridden country.

In the Plaza de Armas I spotted a scruffy-looking internet café and popped in to check my emails. Here I received a robust reminder of an entirely different type of addiction. To avoid retyping 'http' I pulled up the page of the last user. Tattooed foreskins and mammoth pink-and-black boobs with gleaming pierced nipples leaped out at me. At that very moment, the middle-aged, moustachioed café owner walked over to collect my money.

I froze with embarrassment. He looked down at me and smirked. I clumsily explained that I'd gone to the site by accident but he chortled in an 'I've heard that one before' tone, and whispered something to the guy behind the counter who looked over in my direction and winked knowingly. Crimson-faced, I logged out and left.

On my way back to the Don Agucho, I wandered into a dilapidated tour agency. Unsure whether I had the bottle to fly over the Nazca Lines, I let myself be talked into what appeared to be the only other excursion on offer: a visit the next morning to a Nazca graveyard in a place called Chauchilla.

As soon as I left the agency I regretted my impetuous purchase and marvelled at my stupidity. Was I completely nuts? Who, in their right mind, if they were in my situation, would want to visit a graveyard – let alone pay for it? From what I'd seen of Nazca, it looked pretty much like a one-horse town and I was starting to wish I hadn't paid up for two nights.

The cemetery tour involved setting off in yet another battered old Ford taxi which the 'tour company' must have hired; there was no guide, and the only tourists were Greg and me. A lanky, good-looking American in his early thirties, Greg was an attorney from Houston who was taking unpaid leave from his law firm and making his way across South America to Brazil, where he'd lined up a job teaching English in Rio for six months.

En route to the cemetery, our lugubrious taxi driver –

who looked too old to be let loose behind a wheel – made an unannounced diversion to a studio in town where we were given a mandatory demonstration of Nazca pottery-making. It also appeared mandatory, if you valued your life, to buy something in the shop afterwards. I purchased a few stones with Nazca symbols on them, and Greg bought a couple of patterned ceramic plates, which he later regretted as he hadn't a clue how he was going to fit them into his rucksack.

The graveyard was in a scorching desert savannah some thirty kilometres from the town. It was a truly godforsaken place. Scattered around the dusty ground were hundreds of graves, twenty or so recently excavated by archaeologists, and a few more by grave robbers. Skeletons, skulls, hair, fabric and pottery were all exposed to the elements. Thousands of Nazca were buried in these subterranean sepulchres somewhere between the second century BC and the sixth century AD, when their civilisation flourished.

Whole families were seated together in sunken pits, many with dreads down to their waists. Neatly piled up in the corner were cooking pots, bowls and other utensils.

More sinister even than these intimately positioned, relaxed-looking skeleton families were the neat rows of trophy skulls lined up alongside them. The Nazca were famous not only for their desert carvings of geometric lines and images of animals and birds; they also boasted the largest collection of human heads in the Andes. Holes were chiselled into the centre of their enemies' skulls so that a carrying rope could be inserted, once they'd carefully sewn the lips together with long cactus spines.

The heat was intense and, apart from the two of us and the driver, who sat in his cab smoking impatiently and listening to football on a tinny transistor radio, there wasn't a soul around. Nor were there any ticket booths or drink kiosks; just the sunken graves and bits of Nazca bone scattered over the parched plain.

As the only people in the graveyard with flesh on their bodies, a celebratory intimacy ignited between us. Greg agreed with me that the place had a Dali-esque vibe. We cracked black jokes, giggled about the chilled-out skeletons and the uptight driver, and discussed how easy it would be to walk off with some of the unguarded artefacts. Our bottled water was hot, and we both longed, for once, for a kiosk selling ice-cold Coca-Cola. We took our own pictures, then dutifully swapped cameras and took shots of each other. Despite our laughter, we were both starting to feel increasingly uncomfortable around the ghoulish, sun-bleached skulls that were grinning back at us.

Greg wandered off to find somewhere to 'ease himself'. Left alone, I started zoning out on bones and decided that I didn't want to see another one in Peru. These skeletons spooked me more than the bones and skulls I'd stumbled upon in the crypt of the San Francisco monastery in Lima. Death, yet again, was staring me in the face. But in reality it had been doing so for years. When someone close to you is injecting smack, there is no avoiding the fact that you're living in the shadow of death.

The name heroin, ironically enough, is derived from

the German word *heroisch* – which means heroic. This was how the human guinea pigs at the Bayer Pharmaceutical Company in Germany described the substance that was tested on them, and which they found so effective in removing physical and psychological pain. Bayer introduced Heroin Cough Medicine for Children in 1894, marketing it as a non-addictive morphine substitute and cough suppressant. It was considered such a safe and effective medicine that it remained available over the counter until 1914.

There were red faces all round at Bayer when it was discovered that once in the system, heroin actually metabolised rapidly into morphine with more powerful and addictive results. If it were still legal, it would be one of the most effective pain relievers in a doctor's arsenal. Today, however, the word 'heroin' is virtually synonymous with the word 'death'.

I learned that my son was a heroin addict the day after 9/11. David and I had returned from a wet, miserable holiday in Scotland a couple of days earlier, where the only high point had been climbing Ben Nevis. Like millions of others around the world, we were reeling from the seismic shock of the events in New York the day before.

We'd recently moved from Brighton, where David and I had lived since we married, to the Sussex market town of Horsham. Sacha and Rebecca had been redecorating our new home for us while we were in Scotland. Rebecca had already returned to London, leaving Sacha to finish off the painting. David was away filming in Frankfurt.

Sacha and I sipped red wine together and felt close. He said he was proud of me for climbing Ben Nevis and chatted away about his experience of climbing the spectacular Table Mountains in Venezuela's Gran Sabana, which were among the oldest land formations on the planet.

Then he told me he'd been sexually abused at boarding school and that he was a heroin addict.

The abuse admission came as no surprise, but the whispered confession that he was also shooting up heroin completely floored me.

After qualifying as a psychotherapist, I underwent substance misuse training with a drugs and alcohol agency. One of the important facts about heroin that they *didn't* teach on this course was that users come across as 'normal', 'calm' and 'sane' when they're actually on heroin. It's when they're craving it that they look and behave like archetypal junkies.

For years he'd led me to believe he'd experimented once with heroin and that had been it. I thought about the pet rat he'd secretly kept in his drawer as a teenager. He knew that rats and heroin were the stuff of nightmares for me. No wonder he couldn't bring himself to tell me sooner.

There was more bad news to come: Rebecca was on heroin, too.

They'd had to return from Europe because she was experiencing crippling pain in her pelvic region. She went through endless tests, but the pain couldn't be diagnosed. Many – her mother included – wrongly believed it to be psychological in origin, which only increased her desperation. After going several nights without sleep she begged and begged Sacha to let her try some heroin for pain relief. He finally gave in. Her agony subsided but she was immediately hooked.

What he most regretted in his life, Sacha told me, was giving in to Rebecca's pleas to try a bit of smack. Only after Sacha's passing was Rebecca's pain formally diagnosed as being triggered by damaged cutaneous nerves, which are known to send searing pain up through and around the pelvis. She went on to receive the appropriate treatment.

A few months before Sacha's heroin revelation, I'd prevailed upon his father to lend Headflux some money so that Sacha and Rebecca could expand their business. In hindsight, this was a huge mistake. Although they were managing to fill some of their orders, before long they were no longer capable of the day-to-day efficient running of a business. The investment ensured that when their cashflow was low, they could borrow from it to finance their habit. But they always paid back what they owed. Sacha and Rebecca never stole from us, or from anyone for that matter.

Now that I knew Sacha was a junkie, I did all I could to help, but we never seemed to get anywhere. I'd make appointments for him and Rebecca to see health and drug practitioners, but half the time they'd forget or wouldn't turn up. The times when I couldn't get hold of either of them, I was beside myself with worry. My moods and anxiety levels were being governed by theirs; I'd unwittingly become part of the same rollercoaster, and the sense of disempowerment was sometimes agonising.

I wanted to take over Sacha's life, to control it, to get him into rehab whatever it cost. But the more bossy I became, the more he backed off. That old proverb, 'You can take a horse to water, but you can't make it drink', went repeatedly through my head. If only I could get clean for him. The decision to commit to recovery was, I knew, up to the two of them.

I was also well aware of co-dependency issues. Relatives of addicts are often advised to 'release with love' – in other words, to have nothing to do with the user until they get off the drug. But that sort of tough love felt too risky for me. David's exasperation and anger – especially over how Sacha and Rebecca's addiction was affecting me – was starting to surface, but I'd made the decision to be there for them both and I have never regretted it. In Sacha's case, it wasn't only about love. I was also utterly petrified of him dying.

On the taxi ride back into Nazca, Greg and I chatted about the adventures we'd had so far in Peru. He'd flown over the Nazca Lines the day before and was adamant that I should do the same.

'Why?' I asked, knowing full well why.

'Because they're the only reason why any sane person would want to visit this place; they sure as hell wouldn't come for this,' he replied, as we drove past heaps of rubbish piled up on the border of a squatter camp, 'or for the nightmares we'll both be getting from those goddamn skeleton families!'

He was probably right about that last part, but I laughed anyway. Greg rummaged around in his rucksack and fished out a book.

'Here, take this. I don't need it any more.'

He handed me a well-thumbed paperback with the photograph of a wise-faced, wrinkly old woman on the cover. I glanced at the blurb on the back; the book was about a German mathematician called Maria Reiche who had lived beside the Nazca Lines and, until her death in 1998, had spent fifty-two years trying to figure them out.

'Do it, Diane,' Greg said, with an irritated edge to his voice. 'Just do it!'

Unlike the Peruvians I'd met, Greg was refreshingly uncurious as to why I was travelling alone, or how many children I had, and I wasn't about to enlighten him. But I did feel a twinge of sadness when he told me we wouldn't have time to stop for a cold *Cusqueña* because he had to be on the coach to Puno in less than an hour's time; from there he would travel into Bolivia and then on to Brazil.

The taxi dropped him off at the bus station. We exchanged email addresses and said our farewells. As we pulled away I turned around to wave. Greg was standing in the middle of the street, his arms outstretched. He flapped them up and down to emulate airplane wings.

# astronaut and dog

## good grief

Back at the Don Agucho, the receptionist informed me that César had dropped by a couple of hours earlier to see whether I'd made up my mind about the Nazca Lines. Exhausted after the cemetery outing, I was tempted to hide in my room to avoid his predictable reappearance, but it was simply too hot. Instead, I sat on the terrace of the *hacienda* consuming vast quantities of cold mineral water.

In my absence, the hotel owners had put up Christmas decorations. I watched a large red-and-blue parrot peck away at the fake snow on a plastic fir tree that was balancing precariously on the edge of the tiny pool. Whichever hemisphere you happen to find yourself in these days, there is no escaping Christmas.

There was no way of escaping César either. I looked up and saw him walking towards me with a psychedelic grin on his face. Shit! I was going to have to make a decision. We sat together by the pool drinking Fanta. After listening to César extol the virtues of the Nazca Lines for a good thirty minutes, I decided to go for it; partly because I admired his tenacity, but mainly because he'd succeeded in wearing me down.

Handing him a deposit I assured him he could have the remainder of the money when he picked me up at seven the next morning. He warned me not to eat breakfast.

It was way past midnight and too hot to sleep. I lay on my bed in the sweltering room, listening to The Doors on my iPod, watching the ancient wooden ceiling fan going round and round and round. 'The End' started playing; I sniggered when I realised that I must look like a female version of Martin Sheen in the opening sequence of *Apocalypse Now*.

I poured myself a glass of warm Chilean Sauvignon and moved outside. I knew this wasn't a great idea, but I was hoping the wine would help me sleep before I became airborne in a few hours time – unless, that is, I chickened out.

No one was around. Even the cicadas were silent. I liked the silence; it allowed me to think. I slapped away the mosquitoes nibbling my toes and attempted to get to grips with the anxiety I was feeling about the following day's *'gran aventura'*, as César had described it.

My fear about this 'big adventure' was, I realised, partly about being in a small plane. When Sacha was a young child, he and I were trapped for a couple of hours in a London Tube carriage. A woman in our compartment went berserk and tried to smash the door down with her handbag. I remained calm at the time, but had battled with claustrophobia ever since. I'd never let it stop me doing anything or travelling anywhere. Nevertheless, enclosed confined interiors – like the insides of teeny-weeny planes – still panicked me.

Then there was the question of the aircraft itself. How safe would it be? I remembered comforting a friend at university after he'd been given the news that his parents had been killed flying over Peru in a light aircraft. And before leaving England I'd made the mistake of reading a warning on the blog of a recent visitor to the Lines that not all the planes were safe; there had been several fatal crashes in recent years.

But there were worse ways to go, I reasoned to myself. If I did decide to chicken out at the last minute, what would I kick myself for? Just for missing the opportunity to view a World Heritage Site that is purported to be not only one of the most breathtaking archaeological sights in South America, but also the largest artwork in the world – and one of its greatest mysteries.

But the *real* reason I chose to stop off in Nazca in the first place, and why I *had* to fly over the Lines, was because of a conditional promise I'd made my son. It still applied – well, sort of.

We were watching a video documentary about the Sex Pistols. Sacha was lying on a yellow futon in our living room, moaning listlessly. He'd just reached the end of his second 'cluck' – the slang term for coming completely off methadone by reducing the dosage, bit by bit, over ten days – and the methadone bottle was empty. Things weren't looking good; the first cluck hadn't gone well either.

Desperate to get clean, both he and Rebecca had pushed to get onto a methadone programme in London. But Sacha loathed the daily methadone pick-ups that were in some ways as constraining to his freedom as the addiction itself. One day, he decided he wanted to move in with David and me and get clean of the stuff.

But as he started to reduce during that first cluck and the anaesthetising methadone drained out of his body, leg cramps, ulcer pains and the psychological pain of withdrawal made him uncommunicative, restless and depressed. The day he was finally clean, he started crawling the walls in agony. He couldn't stand it and neither could I. But I would have put up with his mood and behaviour for longer if it meant he'd be released from the addiction. While I was out shopping, he called Rebecca and asked her to bring him some smack. A mate of theirs drove her to the house. I was gutted that he'd given in. David was irate.

About six months after this first abortive attempt, Sacha managed to get onto another methadone programme. Before long, he was eager to come back to Horsham and try another home cluck. David, unsurprisingly, wasn't keen on the idea. I looked into the Priory; it was very expensive. I would have re-mortgaged the house if necessary, but the bottom line was that Sacha refused to go into rehab. He'd started to feel paranoid around other people, and the idea of therapy in a group frightened him.

This time, however, Rebecca had decided to come off methadone too. I was optimistic that, with them both wanting to clean up, we had a better chance of succeeding. I sweet-talked David into agreeing. As sick as he was of it all, he also cared a great deal about Sacha and Rebecca. She moved in with their friend Emma, who had offered to support her. David played a lot of golf.

But as we watched the Sex Pistols video at the end of that second cluck, Sacha was once again experiencing acute ulcer pains, and on another massive downer. I was learning, the painful way, that the root of the problem for many junkies was that 'being clean' wasn't the great pinnacle of self-achievement or the entry into a great new life that some non-users imagine it to be. It meant having to face and be tormented by all his inner demons, with no means of escaping them.

I'd naively hoped that the documentary about Sid Vicious and his sad, squalid death from a heroin overdose might motivate Sacha to battle the cravings. But to my disappointment he said it only made them worse. I suppose he identified with the self-destructive behaviour patterns and mindset of another troubled being who had once, like him, inhabited Planet Heroin.

'When you're clean, what would you most like to do?' I asked him.

'See Machu Picchu again and fly over the Nazca Lines,' he responded without hesitation.

'You want to go back to Peru, then?'

'Yeah, I'd really love to take a proper look at the Lines. I only got to see a couple of them from the *mirador*.'

'What's that?'

'A wobbly steel tower about twelve metres high. They built it for skint people like me who can't afford the flight.'

'What could you see from it?'

'Tree, Hand and two halves of Lizard... Pass me my tobacco, Mum.'

'Can't you finish this soup first?'

'Later, Mum, later... Thanks... Can you believe it – they built a fucking highway right through the middle of Lizard? Mad, innit?'

'Once you've been clean for a year, Sacha, I'll pay for you to return to Peru and fly over the Nazca Lines.'

'Cheers, Mum. I really want to see Astronaut and Dog with my own eyes.'

The next day Sacha was in so much pain his mood turned quite obnoxious. He and David almost came to blows, and David stormed off to work. I called the doctor, who, after examining Sacha, arranged for him to be admitted to hospital. My concerned brother Neil immediately left work and came with us.

Even though I'd warned the overworked junior doctor that Sacha had only just completed a methadone detox, the medic stupidly put him on morphine – another opiate – for the pain. When I called the hospital the next day, I was informed that Sacha had discharged himself half an hour earlier.

He rang me from the station not long afterwards, sounding very calm, and said he was about to get on a train back to London. After a very long silence he apologised – profoundly.

When Sacha died a friend of mine commented, 'Death is the greatest adventure of them all.' I was no longer afraid of death, I reasoned, so why be afraid of a small light aircraft? Although it hadn't been achieved in the way I'd hoped, technically speaking, Sacha had been clean for almost a year. I like to keep my promises. He was no longer able to see Astronaut and Dog 'with his own eyes', so I decided I'd better take a look at them for him.

Resisting the temptation to have another glass of wine, I returned to my cooler bed and dreamed about crashing over the Nazca Lines, and being welcomed by Sacha into the light.

We drove to the airport in silence. I said a reluctant goodbye to César as he dropped me off beside a narrow airstrip and pointed to a single-engine, four-seater Cessna plane parked on the runway. The pilot and two passengers were already on board, waiting for the last remaining passenger – me. There could be no backing out now. I clambered into the seat beside the disconcertingly young pilot, who proceeded to manfully strap me in as we introduced ourselves.

'*Tengo miedo*,' I shouted to the young Argentinian couple

seated behind me, as the pilot started up the engine.

'*Yo también,*' the woman shouted back.

I was relieved not to be the only one who was scared. The guy shrugged his shoulders and laughed.

The flimsy plane wobbled along the tiny airstrip, then took off into the cloudless blue sky. We swooped for a few minutes above cratered desert hill formations until a long, high, arid plateau came into view. Anxiety flipped into astonishment as I found myself staring down at one huge geometric puzzle, meticulously positioned in the shadow of the Andes.

Some of the 2,000-year-old lines crisscrossed, others intersected, and a few appeared to head nowhere. The plane glided lower, and it was just possible to see how the removal of the darker brown stones on the surface of the *pampa* had exposed the lighter, reddish-coloured sediment beneath to form the Lines.

Paul Kosok, an American scientist, was the first airborne human to spot the 800 straight lines and 300 geometric and circular shapes when he flew across the desert in 1939. He initially believed they constituted an elaborate irrigation system.

Seven years later, when his visa expired, he asked his young research assistant Maria Reiche – the German mathematician in Greg's book – to take over his work. I had been intrigued to read that when Reiche first sailed to Peru, her ship passed through the centre of four consecutive arched rainbows that touched the waves on either side of the vessel. She believed these awe-inspiring spectrums were a sign that the Nazca Lines were her destiny.

Reiche moved into spartan accommodation in the midst of the Lines, and remained there, mapping and attempting to interpret the celestial matrix of the parched *pampa*, until her death. She claimed the Lines were an astronomical calendar, designed to help the Nazca with planning their planting and harvesting. Not everyone agreed with her, though.

Over the years, there have been numerous alternative theories concerning this bewildering tapestry that covers 500 kilometres of the Pampa Colorado: shamanic flight paths; ancient sacred paths known as *ceques* which were connected to power spots called *huacas*; running tracks for games; landing strips for aliens. Many of the Lines started from a star-like radial point marked by a low mound bordered by rivers and tributaries, which have since dried out. The most recent theory is that they were constructed as sacred walkways to the water that was so precious to the Nazca.

As I stared down at these mysterious patterns in the vast *pampa*, I sensed that Sacha was with me, peering over my shoulder, sharing my excitement as the pilot drew our attention to the many magnificent shapes and designs below: elegant trees and plants, insects, precision-made eternity spirals, human hands. But it was the gigantic zoomorphic geoglyphs gazing up at me that I found most awesome: Hummingbird; Peacock; Spider; Monkey.

I let out an involuntary gasp when Condor, depicted in full flight with its huge wingspan and extended tail feathers and beak, came into view. In Andean mythology the condor was associated with the sun deity and was a symbol of power and good health; these magnificent birds of prey could live for up to seventy years.

A human shape appeared below which seemed to be waving up at us. The pilot told us proudly that this was Astronaut, his favourite, and that he stood thirty metres tall. Astronaut had a space-bubble head; one hand pointed to the sky and the other to the earth.

As the plane circled over Astronaut, it seemed blazingly obvious to me that the Nazca intended their designs to be seen from the sky. *That* was the reason they created them in the first place. They *wanted* to make contact with other possible life in the universe, and for their world to be understood and admired.

I thought back to the alien-like trepanned skulls in Ica Museum; apparently 90 percent of the skulls found around the Lines had been trepanned, too. Perhaps the Nazca *were* visited by aliens after all, and the trepanned skulls an attempt to mimic them?

As enthralling as I found these extraterrestrial possibilities, time was running out and I sensed Sacha's impatience.

'*Dónde está el perro?*' I asked the pilot.

'*El perro no es fácil reconocer,*' he replied.

Anxiety returned. I didn't care if Dog was difficult to recognise, I had to see him.

'*Pero tengo que verlo, por favor!*' I responded, my voice quavering.

We flew over Dog. My Argentinian companions spotted him first and pointed him out to me. The pilot was right; he wasn't easy to identify because there were lines crisscrossing through him. Dog was a weird, skinny-looking creature about fifty metres long with lanky legs and an upright tail. I asked the pilot to swoop around the geoglyph a couple of times so that I could take a closer look.

Archaeologists believed it to be the Peruvian Hairless dog – the popular domestic pet of several ancient Andean civilisations. Because it was vulnerable to sunburn, this bald canine was kept inside during the day but allowed to roam freely at night – earning it the name 'Moonflower Dog'. The Incas believed that stroking the hairless creature could help to ease stomach pains.

How I wish we'd had a Moonflower Dog in my home when Sacha was clucking. Instead we had Dodge and Ruff – Sacha's German Shepherd sister pups. The pups had only just had their injections when he began his first cluck, and, full of hope for the 'new life' ahead, we took them to the nearby woods for their very first walk. My son loved dogs.

When he left home at eighteen, Sacha acquired a girlfriend called Juliette and a lovely Labrador pup he named Bill – soon to grow into an enormous black dog. Bill had attached himself to Sacha at a festival and wouldn't leave him alone. He was covered in cigarette burns so Sacha didn't look too hard to find his original owners. Even though Sacha was the first to admit that Bill wasn't the brightest of dogs, he loved the creature to death. Sadly, he didn't have such intense feelings for Juliette. They split up after Sacha discovered that she'd taken Bill to a festival with a big pink bow tied around his neck.

The Argentinians wanted to take a closer look at Spider. The plane ascended once more and Dog faded into the distance. I was relieved that I'd succeeded in having a good look at both him and Astronaut.

Then it was all over. Too soon for my liking, as my new, fearless self could happily have spent the whole day flying over this captivating landscape. We headed back to the airstrip. After a bumpy landing, I climbed out of the cockpit, elated.

Waiting on the highway for a taxi, I couldn't resist sending a boastful text to David, family and friends. I felt proud of myself and reassured that, despite my grief, I was still able to challenge fear and experience joy and wonder.

Back at the hot *hacienda* that evening, the purple bougainvillea looked luscious against the backdrop of a fading sunset. I sat outside my room reading a text from my sister Sally. She said mine were starting to sound like something out of *The Alchemist* by the cryptic Brazilian writer Paulo Coelho.

I'd recently found this time of day difficult and lonely, but now a welcome peace had descended. I recalled how, for years, Sacha had nagged me to get a dog. But not any old dog, it had to be his favourite pedigree – a Weimaraner.

'Get a Weimaraner, Mum, get a Weimaraner.'

Weimaraners have beautiful silver/gold coats and huge, otherworldly grey eyes. When I cleared out Sacha's flat I found a photograph of a Weimaraner he'd torn out of a magazine and glued onto a sheet of cardboard.

'One day,' I whispered, 'I'll get the dog you've always wanted. I'll call it Nazca.'

# the white city

## the voice hearers

The Royal double-decker pulled into Nazca coach station at 10pm, an hour late as usual, but I didn't mind. I climbed on board, chilled, optimistic and bound for the town of Arequipa. My reserved seat, I was delighted to discover, was upstairs at the very front of the coach and promised a panoramic view in daylight.

Halfway through the nine-hour journey, the coach came to an abrupt standstill in the middle of a desert. I woke up and looked around; from what I could make out in the darkness, the other passengers were still asleep. Had the coach broken down? Had the driver done a runner? The windows, which didn't open, dripped condensation. Black, closed-in, airless; claustrophobic misery loomed. Exactly what I'd dreaded would happen in the Cessna. Thank God I'd brought a torch with me.

I navigated my way – without difficulty – to the malodorous loo downstairs, thinking if I braved it and cleaned my teeth, I might feel more grounded. My strategy failed dismally as the toothbrush fell out of my toilet bag and onto the floor. I binned it immediately.

Back in my seat, I breathed deeply to avert a panic attack. Christ! My two worst fears had buddied up. I'd got myself into some pretty tortuous situations in my life – like agreeing to teach English to a classroom full of Islamic judges, and hanging upside down for a performance at the Institute of Contemporary Arts – but this, being trapped inside a dark, airless tomb in the middle of nowhere with my son's ashes, this *really* took the biscuit.

I began chanting under my breath to summon up some inner strength. It never failed to work. Even during my bleakest times with Sacha, chanting had somehow got me through.

I was introduced to the practice many years ago by a good friend who was about to marry a Buddhist fashion designer. He claimed it had transformed his life. I was hugely sceptical at first, because, as a chronic blamer, I couldn't swallow the idea that you were ultimately responsible for your own karma.

Later the same year, my marriage to Jake broke down and I was almost killed twice while performing ridiculously dangerous airborne stunts with a daredevil performance arts company in London: once from the roof of the Queen Elizabeth Hall and once inside the Bloomsbury Theatre. A nagging voice kept telling me that I wasn't really respecting my life; I was out of rhythm with something – but what?

'A dynamic force known as the Mystic Law,' the designer explained, 'which exists in the universe and in us all.'

When I did, finally, begin to chant, it was for the most unspiritual of reasons.

Celebrating my birthday with a close friend at a wine bar in Holland Park, the good-looking, loaded, Porsche-driving owner of a large computer company invited us to a Chelsea nightclub. There he lavished me with champagne and compliments, and insisted the DJ play all my favourite music. When he dropped me off in the early hours of the morning, he asked for my telephone number and said he'd call in the next day or two, promising wonderful times to come.

Being a girl who, at the time, relied upon men to feel good about herself, I was convinced my luck had changed. But a week later, he still hadn't called. My friend had told me that if I chanted for two weeks, I would receive proof that the practice worked. I went for it.

In that fortnight, I cleared out all my ex's remaining belongings and much of my own tat, redecorated the flat, and felt happier and more centred than I had in a good long time. But when the deadline arrived and Mr Porsche still hadn't made contact, I decided to stop.

The following morning, he called me on his mobile, an impressive, new appendage in those days, while on his way to play rugby. I was flabbergasted; not that after three weeks he'd finally rung, but because I had my proof. And it was when he suggested we meet up 'for din-dins' that I experienced my first moment of enlightenment. *Din-dins!* My arty, bohemian self had absolutely nothing in common with this patronising ex-public schoolboy, who flaunted his class and wealth and hadn't called when he said he would. If I was honest with myself, all I was really interested in was his money, because I didn't have the confidence to believe in my own earning potential as a writer. I thanked him for his invitation and politely declined. From that point on, there was no looking back.

I'd had a very peripatetic childhood and suffered from a sense of rootlessness. My father worked for Unilever and we were constantly on the move. By the age of eleven, I'd attended eight different schools in various parts of England and Ireland. My birth certificate stated that I'd been born at the Red Cross Memorial Hospital in Taplow, near Maidenhead, but I'd never even seen the place.

Some years into my practice, the British branch of the Buddhist organisation moved into its new headquarters at Taplow Court. I was told that the hospital had once been part of the grounds. The centre was impressive, and the surrounding countryside was lush and tranquil. I'd come home at last.

Whenever I'd faltered, my son's dramas had kick-started me back into practising Buddhism. His death had been the biggest challenge to my practice. But then Buddhism was also about learning to transform the 'four sufferings of life' – birth, old age, sickness and death. I still had a long way to go with that last one.

I took out the paperback I was reading by a fellow Soka

Gakkai Buddhist, Mariane Pearl. Mariane's American Jewish husband, Daniel Pearl, was the South Asia bureau chief of *The Wall Street Journal*. Daniel was kidnapped in 2002 while investigating the case of the shoe bomber Richard Reid and the alleged links between Al Qaeda and Pakistan's Inter-Services Intelligence. Daniel's captors beheaded him.

Mariane described her torment in *A Mighty Heart* – a book that later became a movie starring Angelina Jolie. I found her courage in the face of such suffering formidable: 'Terrorists may have destroyed my husband, but they will not have the satisfaction of destroying me.' I decided, then, that Sacha's death wouldn't destroy me either – and that there were more important things to angst about than being stuck in a dark, stuffy bus for a couple of hours.

To my immeasurable relief the engine eventually started up again. I dozed off until the sun came streaming in through the windows in front of me, and I was treated to a glorious vista of spectacular high passes, statuesque rock formations, giant boulders and deep canyons. I listened to *Madame Butterfly* on my iPod and had a virtual epiphany as I sipped sweet black coffee and watched albino clouds sweep across violet mountains. At last I was reaping the benefits of travelling by road.

Years ago, rather than fly, I opted to take a coach journey across Colombia with Sacha's father, Roberto. That landscape, like this one, was stunning. We travelled from Barranquilla on the coast to Medellín in the mountains. The journey was long and arduous, but the views made it worthwhile. Some images continue to haunt me. Once, we were passing through a badly flooded region bathed in a breathtaking sunset. In the absence of a skull and crossbones sign, someone had tied a dead dog to an electricity pylon as a warning. I found the scene perversely beautiful. In such a poverty-stricken, illiterate region the gesture was essentially a benevolent, life-saving one.

Although already a mother, I was also a young, barely travelled student. I'd been holed up in posh country clubs around Barranquilla with wealthy in-laws for a couple of weeks, so this trip was a huge eye-opener. I finally got to see more of the country. Cock fights in the middle of nowhere. *Putas* – prostitutes – of all ages, shapes and sizes. Men so drunk on *aguardiente* that they pissed in their pants before falling into their cars and driving home. The word *machismo* originated in Colombia, and the Colombian guys I came across, Roberto included, certainly felt they had to live up to their reputations.

The Royal coach pulled into Arequipa at 8am. I was disappointed that I was unable to see the famous, ice-capped volcano, El Misti, which towered over this second largest city in Peru, because it was too, er, misty.

Nicknamed the White City because of the light, volcanic

rock from which it was built, Arequipa got its name from the Quechua phrase *'ari quepay'* – meaning 'OK, let's stop here.' That is what the fourth Inca emperor, Mayta Capac, was supposed to have said to his generals when he stopped off on his way back from Cusco. Pizarro also took a liking to the place and 'founded' it in 1540, calling it Villa Hermosa (Beautiful Town).

I booked into an enchanting, higgledy-piggledy hotel on the outskirts of town called La Casa De Mi Abuela. My room in My Grandmother's House was minuscule and a bit shabby, but hammocks had been strung between the trees in the manicured, walled garden, and it had the cleanest swimming pool I'd seen so far in Peru. Too exhausted to swim, I lay down on the faded satin bedspread with the intention of reading – but promptly fell asleep.

Six hours later I woke up in the dark, hungry and shivering with cold. Having finally adjusted to the scorching heat of Nazca, I wasn't ready for this massive drop in temperature. La Casa De Mi Abuela's restaurant was even chillier – and gloomy with it. The waitress grew increasingly irritated as I moved around from table to table, trying to find one that was draught-free. The *paella*, when it finally arrived, wasn't worth the long wait. On my way out, I tipped the piano player who made this mediocre gastronomic event just about bearable, and who looked as cold and forlorn as me.

I was surprised to see, when I glanced in the bathroom mirror the next morning, that I looked good for a change: no eye bags, healthily tanned. I also felt calmer, more centred

– more myself. Maybe I was just relieved that I wouldn't be on the road for a couple of days, stressing out about baggage and coach drivers. I was way up in the desert mountains of the Andes, some 2,500 metres above sea level. Perhaps it was Sacha's peace I was sensing as we made our ascent. Arequipa has a similar altitude to Machu Picchu. The first anniversary of his passing was only a couple of weeks away now.

As I ambled towards the centre of this high-elevation city, my limbs started to feel weirdly heavy, and as for my head, it felt like a balloon. This wasn't an altogether unpleasant sensation, simply a curious one.

Arequipa was indeed a white city. Constructed out of sillar, a white volcanic stone, the imposing Spanish colonial buildings gleamed above my dreamy altitude head; I was inside a fairytale citadel. I meandered along, paying little attention to where I was going.

The city was totally destroyed by earthquakes and volcanic eruptions in 1600. Since then Arequipa has been pulverised on a regular basis, the latest quake being in 2001. Thankfully, many of the impressive old colonial buildings and churches survived, but, alas, Beautiful Town, so the guide book informed me, also had its fair share of strangle-muggings.

Towering over the city were two gloriously white spires and it made sense to head for them. The spires crowned an immense cathedral, whose façade dominated an entire side of Arequipa's Plaza de Armas. I entered warily: the cathedral was gutted by fire in 1844 and then destroyed by an earthquake in 1868. One of its towers fell down in the 2001 quake.

Inside the basilica the aisles and altars were adorned with gladioli. Feeling totally spaced out I slumped into the first available pew. From there I admired the cathedral's baroque décor and intricate gold work. There was a sizeable congregation, but no sign of a service about to begin.

In other cathedrals and churches, I'd seen Peruvians, from grandmothers to young kids, coming and going all day long to pray, some attending Mass several times a day. But the people here appeared to have a different agenda. Only a few were praying; others were staring exhaustedly at the altar; a number were asleep. Judging by their threadbare, soiled clothes, what they had in common was poverty. The clean, dry cathedral clearly provided a temporary sanctuary from the pavement or from their overcrowded, leaking corrugated-iron shacks.

Sanctuary was what I attempted to provide for Sacha and Rebecca as 2002 drew to a close. They were still living in squats, and I realised they needed a stable base from which to sort out their chaotic lives and access the necessary services to get healthy and clean. I decided to buy a flat and rent it out to them; the rent would help pay for the mortgage. We all agreed on Brighton. They were both enthusiastic. Sacha came down from London several weekends in a row and we went flat-hunting together. Eventually, we found a one-bedroom garden flat, conveniently close to the Downs for walking the dogs.

On a warm April afternoon, I picked up the keys from the estate agent. Sitting on the steps leading up to the garden with the sun on my face, I looked around at the spring flowers, the cherry tree coming into blossom, the sea sparkling below. I breathed a sigh of relief that Sacha, Rebecca and the dogs had a proper roof over their heads at last.

My reverie was disturbed by a very old priest who shuffled up to me, shakily grasped my hand, and welcomed me to Arequipa. I asked him why there were so many vases of gladioli in the cathedral. These resplendent orange blooms, he explained, were a traditional Christmas decoration in churches all over Peru.

He was eager to know my name and where I was from. His kindness touched me and was a reminder that I was in a place of worship, not a museum. I put my camera away and wobbled to my feet. He offered to show me around. I accepted the antique arm he proffered, and as we stumbled down the aisle together he recounted the dramatic history of the 450-year-old cathedral.

The altitude hit me again when I ventured outside. I sat down on the cathedral steps and watched as passers-by threw coins into the hats or onto the blankets of beggars who were slumped against the railings. The crippled and the blind were more fortunate recipients than the deranged-looking ones. The world over, the physically afflicted appear to receive more cash and compassion than the mentally afflicted. I gave some coins to a legless old woman in a wheelchair of sorts, and to a mumbling young man with matted hair and wild eyes sitting a few steps below me. It could, at one time, have been Sacha.

I'm back in Brighton, at the Priory clinic. Sitting opposite me is the sombre, empathic psychiatrist who has just assessed my son. I booked the private consultation in desperation. The psychiatrist diagnoses schizophrenia. He says it has been triggered by Sacha's history of sexual abuse.

Sacha seems relieved that his condition is out in the open. For years, he tells us, he's been hearing aggressively critical voices in his head. The only way he can drown them out, he says, is through self-medicating. Heroin has been the first drug that has really and truly shut the voices up, but when he isn't using they're amplified. The psychiatrist says this is a familiar story and prescribes anti-psychotic medication.

This depressing new development had taken me by surprise as life seemed to be looking up for Sacha and Rebecca. They were excited about the move to Brighton, Headflux had also taken off again, they were earning more money and using only infrequently. Or so they told me.

The night before they were due to move, Sacha had loaded their possessions into a van in London. But the next morning, Rebecca called to say that Sacha had disappeared with the dogs in the early hours and wasn't answering his phone. Eventually he called, but he wasn't making sense. He said he was in trouble; women wearing wigs of different colours were following him around and it wasn't safe for him to return to Rebecca. Some hours later he appeared on my doorstep in Horsham with the dogs, frightened, exhausted, staring into space and mumbling.

Rebecca drove the van down and we moved their stuff into the Brighton flat late that night. The 'sanctuary' I thought I'd provided them with was destined to become the setting for yet more heartache.

The wild-eyed, mumbling young beggar emptied the contents of his cap into his pockets and slowly descended the steps of the cathedral. Others like him took his place and began eyeing me up. I couldn't face or afford another onslaught. It was time to make a move.

Descending the cathedral steps I could hear the strains of a harmonica. I looked around. Leaning against a wall for support, an old Quechua man, wearing a bleached Panama hat and a seriously frayed Western suit, was playing a melancholy blues tune. The chords pierced my heart. I was reminded of Sacha's harmonica playing and his virtuoso renditions of the blues.

In the hope of lifting my bluesy mood, I jumped into a taxi and asked to be taken to Yanahuara church in the suburbs of

Arequipa, reputedly of great historical interest as it housed the 'highly venerated Virgen de Chapi'. According to my guide book, the church opened at 3pm but when I arrived at 4pm, I found a notice on the door saying it was closed until 6.30pm. My main reason for deciding to visit the church was because it was also an observation point for the El Misti volcano. But El Misti was still covered in mist.

As I waited for a taxi to take me back to the hotel, a couple of cheeky teenagers juggling potatoes in the middle of a zebra crossing brought a welcome smile to my face; they were laughing away at the red-faced, hooting drivers leaning out of their cars in the long line of traffic the kids were holding up.

My Grandmother's House no longer enchanted me. At night, it was bursting at the seams with Christmas-season tourists. I sat by the decent-sized pool, conscious that my enthusiasm for children was also fast ebbing away. I longed for a dip, but the pool had been invaded by a loudmouthed French woman with the biggest bum this side of the Atlantic and her five shrieking, dive-bombing progeny.

When Sacha died, my poor mother searched desperately to find words to console me. She eventually came up with, 'You know, darling, you should be grateful that at least you've had the experience of motherhood; some unlucky women can't have children.' As I lay on the lounger, getting regularly splashed by this rowdy Gallic rabble, I caught myself wondering whether these progeny-deficient women really were so unlucky.

I was exceedingly pissed off with Sacha when, after I'd done all I could to help him acquire a stable base in Brighton and a more stable head, I discovered that he and Rebecca were spending most of their time up in London and that he was often 'forgetting' to take the anti-psychotic medication the psychiatrist had prescribed. The tablets, Sacha complained, had the side-effect of making him sleep much of the time, and of generally numbing and dumbing him down.

According to Sacha, they were in London because they had to get their car fixed. I, meanwhile, was running around Brighton, getting estimates for new windows and doors and having fences put up so that the dogs didn't jump into neighbours' gardens. He later confessed that they'd started using heavily again after hearing about the death of a friend, and had been staying with other friends in London while attempting yet another cluck.

It finally sank in that, as with most addicts, any conflict or drama would be a reason – or an excuse – for them to kick-start their habit again. This time, it was losing a friend. And I'd been naïve enough to think that providing a home would be sufficient motivation for Sacha and Rebecca to begin to really tackle their problems and turn their lives around.

It was around this time that I wrote to Sacha: 'I feel I have two sons – 1) the messed up, aggressive, nasty/paranoid/selfish, alcho/junkie – and 2) the intelligent, warm Sacha, who loves his family/his partner/his dogs, wants to study history, computers, whatever, continue travelling the world and have a happy life.'

In a child-unfriendly mood, I left the pool and headed for the convent of Santa Catalina, one of the main tourist attractions in Arequipa. The nunnery consisted of mazes, cloisters, tiny plazas, large impressive halls with vaulted ceilings and narrow paths which twisted and turned. Its courtyards and terraces had been artfully mosaic-patterned, and the outside walls brightly painted in an assortment of colours.

The mayor of Arequipa forced the convent to modernise in 1970 and open its doors to tourism; now only thirty nuns resided there. Although the nuns' rooms were small and fairly austere, there was a surprisingly joyful atmosphere inside the convent.

As I mooched around, fantasising about what it would be like to live a childfree, cloistered existence, I couldn't help suspecting that perhaps Santa Catalina hadn't always been child-free. Founded by a rich widow in 1580 for husbandless daughters of some of the best Spanish conquistador families, convent life at Santa Catalina wasn't the usual one of chaste poverty. The nuns invited musicians into the convent, held parties, and had between one and four servants or slaves each, the majority of whom were black, according to records.

The fun and games went on until the 19th century, when a killjoy pope got to hear about the wild goings-on at Santa Catalina and decided enough was enough. He sent one Josefa Cadena, a strict Dominican sister, to put a stop to it all. She freed the servants and slaves and stamped out the partying. From that point on, the nuns rarely left the walls of the convent.

After two hours of milling around the cloisters I was more than ready to escape. I also craved caffeine to jolt me out of my altitude daze.

Most of the clientele in the arty, book-strewn café where I enjoyed a double helping of strong Peruvian cappuccino appeared to be deep in discussion. Arequipeños pride themselves on their intellectual and political savviness. One of the most influential Latin American writers, the Nobel Prize-winning novelist and right-leaning politician, Mario Vargas Llosa, was born in the White City.

And so, for that matter, was Abimael Guzmán – alias Comrade Gonzalez, the leader of Sendero Luminoso (Shining Path) – the brutal Maoist insurgents who all but crippled Peru from the late 1970s until 1992, when this psoriasis-suffering, former Kantian philosopher and university professor was peacefully arrested – above a ballet studio in Lima, of all places.

A couple in their early thirties lugging bags crammed full of what looked like the weekly shop pushed a twin buggy containing identical twin girls into the café. They sat down at my table, lit up cigarettes and ordered ice cream. Mum and dad, both lithe, intense-looking *mestizos,* could have passed for twins too. They saw me reading my guide book, smiled warmly, and asked me if I was from the States.

The little twins shyly whispered their names to me – Lila and Luz. Despite their shining black ringlets and mahogany eyes, Lila and Luz were not quite as angelic as they looked. Banging their spoons on the table and smearing ice cream in each other's hair, they let out high-pitched cries and shrieks, to the consternation of the café staff.

Their parents, Patricio and Daniela, were more interested in talking politics than in policing their twins. Both were secondary school teachers in the city; she taught biology and he taught history. I was surprised to hear that, since I'd been in the country, a state of emergency had been declared in six provinces following the murder of eight policemen, apparently by Sendero Luminoso. I hadn't realised the group was still active, and wondered if that explained the centre-right demonstration I'd stupidly tried to photograph in Lima before getting a police baton waved in my face.

Sendero Luminoso, Daniela told me, had been responsible for more than half the 70,000 deaths which had occurred during the insurgency. Patricio dolefully lit another cigarette and said that he'd lost an uncle – a local government officer – in army crossfire. The figure 70,000 reverberated in my brain like a wake-up call. All those deaths. All those bereaved families. I wasn't alone here. I needed to get my own loss into perspective.

Attempting to lighten the doleful mood that had descended, I asked them if they'd heard of another Lila – Lila Downs – the Mexican/American-Scottish singer/

songwriter who has a smoky, sonorous voice and bears an uncanny resemblance to Frida Kahlo. They hadn't, so I let them listen to some of *Una Sangre* on my iPod. They nodded politely, and then went straight back to discussing politics.

Did I know that Alberto Fujimoro, the former president, had been arrested in Chile last month and was likely to go to prison for corruption under his watch? I shook my head, embarrassed at my lack of interest in their country's politics. I'd always kept abreast of what was happening in Latin America and elsewhere, but for the past year I'd been so busy wading around in the swamp of my grief that I'd let the world pass me by.

Thankfully, I'd heard of Alejandro Toledo, the centre-left current president and the first of Indigenous origin since Peru achieved independence in the early 19th century. Patricio liked him more than Daniela did: there had been talk of electoral fraud. He was cleared, but she remained slightly suspicious. Half of all Peruvians are of pure Quechan blood, Patricio told me, and the remainder, Spanish or *mestizo*: it was about time that an Indigenous Peruvian got a shot at the presidency.

Neither of them had a good word to say about the patrician Vargas Llosa. After he'd challenged Fujimoro for the presidency in 1990, and lost, he'd given Peru, the country of his birth, the finger, and taken up Spanish citizenship. Patricio and Daniela seemed more upset by this Arequipan's 'betrayal' of his city than by his politics.

I could have happily chatted away to this charismatic

couple for longer, but the twins would have none of it, and started making such a racket that Patricio and Daniela decided to leave the café before they were asked to. Caffeine-fuelled, I wandered around the streets and enjoyed dipping in and out of politically orientated galleries, bookshops and gaudy designer emporiums, soaking up the mixture of wild Latino and conservative Gringo vibes that typified Arequipa.

I couldn't face eating in the restaurant again that evening, so I sat in Grandmother's tiny cell/bedroom, nibbling some bread, cheese and grapes I'd purchased earlier. Feeling lonely after my meagre supper, I hunted around for the remote to switch on the battered-looking portable television in the corner. Sacha used to have the television on almost constantly once Rebecca left, as an antidote to loneliness.

Although Rebecca loved her mother and father, who lived in the Midlands, relations between them were often strained. She had begged me not tell them that she was taking heroin. Her mother rang me from time to time, anxious for news of her daughter. I was in a very difficult position. What if Rebecca overdosed and the unspeakable happened? Surely, I argued with myself, her parents had a right to know their daughter was an addict. Even if they didn't want to do anything about it, at least I would be giving them the choice. But telling them could also jeopardise my relationship with Rebecca.

Matters came to a head when I visited Brighton one day. Rebecca was in bed and I was shocked to see how dreadful she looked: thin, pale, depressed and in pain with her still undiagnosed health problem. I drove home, rang her mother and told her that Rebecca and Sacha were heroin addicts.

It was a painful call to have to make, but Rebecca and her parents have since thanked me, many times, for making it. A couple of days later she was admitted to hospital in Brighton. I rang Rebecca's mother again and her parents drove down immediately. She was discharged from hospital into their care. They took her very briefly to the Brighton flat so that she could collect a few clothes, then back home. And that was the last time Rebecca and Sacha ever saw each other.

Rebecca was immediately put on a drugs programme. Her parents insisted, understandably, that they would only support her in her recovery if she stopped seeing Sacha. But her departure was catastrophic for him. He began spending more and more time with friends in London. When he was in Brighton or staying with me, all he seemed inclined to do was listlessly play games on his PlayStation or watch television.

Grandmother's television was kaput. Fortunately for me, reading has always been a preferable antidote to loneliness.

I lay on the bed with David Mitchell's *Cloud Atlas,* listening to the soft, sweet sounds of young children chatting and giggling together in the hotel gardens below – so different to the aggressive screeching of the pool terrorists and the little twins' lachrymose squeals earlier in the day. I decided that my mother was probably right. In spite of all I'd had to go through with Sacha, I was glad I hadn't missed out on the experience of motherhood.

After speaking with other mothers who have lost children, I've come to the conclusion that, in the final analysis, your child's destiny, fate, karma – whatever you want to call it – is ultimately their own, and you can't change it, even though you would happily give your life to do so. All that you can do is be there with them, for them, in their suffering. As Khalil Gibran, author of *The Prophet,* says: 'Your children are not your children.'

# staying afloat

## a carer's life

On my last morning in Arequipa, the alarm went off at sunrise. I scrambled out of bed, threw on my clothes and flew out of the door. Outside, the sky was clear and I was able, at last, to admire the city's main landmark – the magnificent, ice-capped volcano, El Misti.

This was followed by a breakneck taxi run to the bus station, courtesy of a driver who was twenty-five minutes late, rambled on about how he'd been written up in some ancient *Lonely Planet* guide, and then proceeded to grossly overcharge me. I didn't have time to argue because the coach was leaving in ten minutes. Or so I'd been led to believe.

Once inside the bus station, true to form, I discovered that I'd been given the wrong time again. The Royal coach wasn't leaving for another hour, and – surprise, surprise – I wasn't on the hostess's reservations list. Fortunately, there was one seat left, window seat number 7; lucky number 7. But I very nearly wasn't so lucky.

Just as the coach was about to pull away, an official came on board and informed me that I needed to pay a bus station tax at the office. Panic set in, but I wasn't alone. A couple of other Gringos on the coach were in the same boat. We legged it to the office, only to discover that it hadn't yet opened. A sweet-seller directed us to the bus station lavatory, where we forked out no small sum to the attendant, who handed us dodgy-looking 'tourist only' tickets in return. We ran back to the bus and managed to jump on just before it pulled away.

The Andean landscape between Arequipa and Puno was arresting. Llamas and alpacas elegantly grazed its rocky hillsides and fertile plains. But it was the Indigenous people in their bold, bowler hat-like *sombreros* and ear-flap *chullo* caps haggling away at roadside market stalls that really captured my attention. Many of the women were dressed in brightly patterned, hand-woven skirts known as *polleras*, and the men sported colourful ponchos whose design depicted their village. Only a handful wore jeans and baseball caps. At last, I was seeing more of Quechua Peru.

Seated beside me on the coach was an athletic-looking guy of Hispanic descent, who was reading a Spanish translation of Milan Kundera's *The Unbearable Lightness of Being*. I wanted to tell him it was one of my favourite books, but I was annoyed with him for being so disgruntled when I'd politely asked him, as we were leaving Arequipa, to move out of my window seat. The hostile silence between us affected me. Sudden loss had made me acutely conscious of how unbearably light our existence actually is, and of wanting to live without regrets. Such petty strops between strangers kill the possibility of what might perhaps be an interesting conversation.

The coach turned into the town of Puno and my neighbour reached up for his rucksack. I seized the opportunity to clear the air by asking him, in Spanish, if he lived in Puno.

'No', he replied rather haughtily in English, 'I am visit my fiancée in the university.'

The hostess announced that soon the driver would be taking a two-hour break before continuing to Cusco and suggested that, if we weren't disembarking, we take the opportunity to do some sightseeing. I asked the young man what there was to see in Puno.

'The cathedral is of interesting,' he replied, after a long pause. 'There is carving of *sirenas* playing guitar on outside.'

*Sirenas?*

'They have one body of woman from here.' He indicated his upper torso. 'And tail of fish the remaining.'

'Ah! Mermaids!'

'Sí. The local peoples,' he said, with a hint of derision in his voice, 'think mermaids swims in the lake and their beautiful songs drown the mans who fish it.'

The coach turned a corner and a vast expanse of turquoise water came into view. Puno itself didn't look anything special but it happened to be positioned on the shores of Lake Titicaca, the highest navigable lake in the world – also famed for making generations of schoolboys titter in geography lessons. For the Incas, Titicaca had a more sacred reputation. Legend had it that the world was created when the god Viracocha rose out of Titicaca and created the sun, moon, stars, and the very first human beings. They believed that the original Inca himself, King Manco Capac, was born here.

Quite how the local people had acquired Homer's siren myth – or whether it was authentically their own – baffled me. But there was no time to question my coach companion further as he was busy waving to a pretty girl in jeans and an 'I love Shakira' T-shirt standing at the lakeside coach stop.

'*Hasta luego*,' he muttered, shoving the book into his rucksack, and sprinting off the coach and into her arms.

My own 'nice to meet you' fell on deaf ears. At least I tried.

For a few moments I stared out at the lake, uncertain what to do. I hadn't anticipated this stop, but now I was here, I was more interested in taking a look at a couple of the forty or so Islas Flotantes – floating islands made from reeds – I'd read about than visiting Puno's cathedral.

The Uros tribe began constructing these islands hundreds of years ago to hide from the aggressive Collas inhabitants in the region, as well as the Inca taxman. Some two thousand or so Uros people still reside on the lake. Not only had they succeeded in outwitting the Incas with their floating tax-havens, they'd also managed to outlive them.

I made my way over to the pier where I'd spotted a couple of tour boats filling up with tourists. I was disappointed to learn that they offered only two- or three-hour trips around the islands – neither of which would work for me. But huddled around a nearby jetty was an assortment of battered wooden rowing boats and fat-looking canoes made of reeds. Every vessel had an animal head on its mast.

Weatherbeaten, smiling faces beamed up at me, each of their owners offering a ride out to the floating islands. The nearest islands, these Uros boatmen assured me, were only half an hour's row away. I was about to opt for a tatty but safe-looking wooden rowing boat with a red-and-black puma head on the mast when it occurred to me that the reed canoes were probably faster. I paid for an hour-long tour with a muscular rower. I didn't want the coach to leave without me.

The canoe almost seesawed over when I stepped onboard and squatted tentatively down on a patterned reed mat. A fierce-looking masthead with reed fangs glared down at me. It could have been a dragon, or a Rottweiler. You can't be too precise with reeds.

The boatman pushed off from the jetty and I contemplated, with a thumping heart, the unbearable lightness of reeds and whether this impetuous jaunt would prove a huge mistake on my part. My rower's name failed to reassure me on this point. It *sounded* like *Quizás* – which means 'Maybe' in English – but perhaps I'd misheard him. Spanish was a second language for us both. He motioned for me to relax and lean back onto a couple of water-soiled reed cushions in the stern.

Quizás was a swift rower. He needed to be. Titicaca is fifteen times the size of Lake Geneva. A number of his teeth were missing and his eyes had almost disappeared inside the creases lining his face. Oily, black hair straggled his shoulders. If it weren't for his barbecued complexion he could have passed for an Inuit.

I'd have liked to ask him what it was like living on a floating island, and how it felt to close your eyes at night not knowing where you'd wake up in the morning, but he was focused so intently on the oars that I didn't want to disturb him. Instead, I recalled how, not that long ago, I used to open my eyes and wonder what I'd woken up to that day – and I knew it wouldn't be anything as calming and lovely as Lake Titicaca.

Rebecca had sorted out a fair amount of the detritus of Sacha's life – much more than I'd realised – and once she was out of the picture, it was all down to me. Some days I had difficulty staying afloat. Other days I felt I was drowning.

I wasn't sure who I was any more. On the surface, I presented myself as a caring, efficient psychotherapist/writer, with some successful plays and TV scripts behind her, married to a charming, biker-mad guy who worked in television.

But this woman's *doppelgänger* was a frightened, exhausted mother who spent hours driving up and down the A23 between her home and Brighton, walking boisterous dogs, putting on plastic gloves to clear up dirty needles behind her son's bed, and waiting around with him for hours at the drug clinic in a room full of depressed junkies, before driving home again to pay her partner some much-needed attention. It almost came as a relief one day when an addict whom Sacha was chatting to in the waiting room was amazed to learn that I was his mother and not his partner. Thank God, I remember thinking, I don't look too old yet.

The crazy thing about stress is that when you're experiencing it you have a tendency to take on more stuff, rather than less. I was, in retrospect, unnecessarily anxious that David wouldn't see Sacha as a drain on our finances, and I said yes to more and more work.

Besides working at a private London clinic, seeing, among a variety of clients, some celebrities, members of the establishment and wealthy bankers, I was also working as a consultant at a family mental health charity in Lewisham where the majority of service-users were poor women of various nationalities. The charity started up a sister project in a small town in Kent where a number of deprived families from London were being relocated and I agreed to do some consultancy work for them, too.

Sometimes it was a welcome relief to lose myself in the problems of others; to remember that I wasn't the only person alive who was going through hell. Most of the time when I was working, Sacha went into another part of my brain. But at other times, particularly when I was dealing with abused and addicted clients, I couldn't help but remember that I had one at home myself.

My local adult education centre asked me to run a confidence-building programme. More unhappy women –

– but middle-class this time, and too embarrassed to admit they were suffering from anxiety and panic attacks. I had also stupidly let the centre talk me into teaching a weekend workshop on scriptwriting. They wanted me back to repeat both classes but, by this time, I'd come to my senses. It had finally dawned on me that I'd become a workaholic.

I was also under commission to write a London stage play about mermaids. Writing was my one area of real escape. The deadline became urgent. I tried to get my imagination to work, tried to submerge myself in water, in the ocean, but I was simply too dried out.

I asked Quizás if it was true that there were mermaids in the lake. He nodded his head.

'Sí, hay sirenas,' he said, with a twinkle in his eye.

I wanted to know if he'd seen any himself.

'Sí, pero las dos veces que estaba borracho.'

Yes, he told me, he'd seen them twice – when he was drunk. I burst out laughing. Chortling away, he added that 'los locos' – crazy ones – also believed there were cities of silver and gold under the water.

In the distance, on the Bolivian side of the lake, I could see the snow-capped Cordillera Real Mountains, which included some of the highest peaks in the Andes. The altitude here was higher than Arequipa but it didn't seem to affect me. I closed my eyes and breathed in the delicious air – possibly the purest my Western lungs had ever encountered – and listened to the gentle, hypnotic lapping of water against the side of the canoe.

Almost two years ago to the day, I'd fallen asleep while being rowed around another tranquil, mirror-like, island-dotted lake.

David had taken me to Sri Lanka for a much-needed break. We wanted to explore the ancient Sinhalese site of Polonnaruwa but hadn't realised that, over the traditional New Year pilgrimage season, thousands upon thousands of Sri Lankans were also making their way there. We arrived in our hire car late in the evening, almost out of petrol, only to discover there were no filling stations or vacant hotel rooms.

We drove round and round the lake, but the only decent accommodation still available cost $250 a night. Almost out of fuel, we ended up staying in a disgustingly overpriced, opportunistic hovel called the Green Shadow. The loo was broken, the grimy bedding infested, the water and electricity cut off at night. The next morning, exhausted and flea-bitten, we eventually managed to find a petrol station and made our way to the Polonnaruwa site.

Polonnaruwa itself struck us as fairly unremarkable, until we came across the Gal Vihara (Stone Shrine) consisting of four enormous ancient Mahayana Buddhas, beautifully carved out of stone. I was mesmerised by the famous 14-metre-long, reclining Buddha, which emanated a gentle air of transcendent grandeur. There were very few people around, so we climbed onto a nearby rock and did our morning chant and recitation of a portion of the Lotus Sutra. As I stared into the Buddha's face, I had a very real and profound sense of the eternity of life. And I thought intensely about Sacha.

Our unplanned pilgrimage brought us unexpected good fortune because, an hour later, we came across a wonderful, inexpensive hotel with a great pool and a fine view of Lake Giritale. It was called the Royal Lotus, and it couldn't have been more different to the Green Shadow. Chilled and happy, we spent the afternoon exploring the placid, breezeless lake, its shores replete with monkeys, elephants and other wildlife. Sadly, the peace I felt while being rowed around Lake Giritale didn't stretch as far as England.

I hadn't wanted to leave Sacha on his own over Christmas and we'd agreed that he would stay with my parents while the dogs would go into kennels – which my father had offered to pay for. Sacha rang the moment we got back home in a terrible state. He hadn't, at the last minute, been able to bring himself to put the dogs into kennels because he thought it cruel, and had ended up spending Christmas on his own in some squat in London.

I drove up to London to meet him. He was so pleased to see me. I was heartbroken to see him. He hadn't been taking his medication and was also very ill with a bronchial infection. Worse still, he confessed he was really missing Rebecca and had started using once more. With David's agreement, Sacha and the dogs moved in with us again.

I managed, with great difficulty, to get him onto another

methadone programme in Brighton and bought him a season ticket so he could travel from my home in Horsham down to Brighton each day to collect his medication. I also encouraged him to re-engage with the Community Mental Health Team to whom the psychiatrist had referred him. He was put on an Advanced Care Plan Approach, for those receiving care in the community. I became his named carer.

After a lovely respite in Sri Lanka I had been thrown back, yet again, into the unbearable heaviness of being.

A couple of small, floating islands appeared on the horizon. Smoke was drifting up from one of them. Alarmed, I asked Quizás if the island was on fire. He laughed and said no, they were cooking their lunch. I was curious to know why an island made of reeds didn't go up in flames. The fires were built on a bed of stones, he explained.

I glanced at my watch. The coach was due to leave in less than an hour. Registering my nervousness about rowing much closer, Quizás produced a small pair of binoculars and stuck two fingers up at me. I handed him two sol. Through scratched lenses I was able see fishermen bobbing up and down in reed boats on the water, and a few wigwams and Neolithic-looking reed structures on the islands themselves. A couple of homes had sloping reed roofs with solar panels. I also spotted the odd television aerial.

A cormorant was tethered to a post on the edge of one of the islands. Quizás told me that lazy islanders used them to catch fish. There were a few cats around to perform a similar duty with the rats. Although I couldn't see any, I could hear several dogs barking.

The islands are woven out of the tough *totora* reeds that grow in the lake. Although reeds are an environmentally sustainable building material, the chief downside of using them is that they rot quickly when they're underwater, so new reeds have to be continually matted into the surface. On a couple of the islands I could see women in brightly coloured skirts and bowler hats, weaving away to keep their islands afloat as chickens and children romped around them.

As his carer, I'd worked tirelessly to keep my son afloat. But as soon as one element of 'rot' in his life had been eliminated, yet another would inevitably surface.

Although he was managing to keep off hard drugs, the chaos and confusion around Sacha didn't abate. I spent hours cleaning his flat and washing his clothes. I'd accompany him to the drug clinic, the doctor, the dentist and the mental-health unit. I wrote endless letters and made umpteen phone calls to mental-health and drug psychiatrists, psychiatric nurses and to his GP to make sure he was getting the best help available.

I wrote to magistrates' courts when he'd been caught on the train without a ticket, and filled out court mitigation forms when, for example, it became clear he hadn't paid his television licence. I had endless, brain-numbing conversations with mobile-phone call centres in India to get his bills sorted and his lost phones replaced. As his carer, I had to explain to them that he was mentally ill and suffering from diminished responsibility.

I was looking after the dogs too, because, as much as he wanted to, Sacha was often too sick or feeling too paranoid to sort them out. I bulk-purchased their food from Pets At Home, venting displaced anger at its ridiculous name. Where the fuck else were pets supposed to be? At Work? When Dodge and Ruff were sick, I drove them and Sacha to the People's Dispensary for Sick Animals (PDSA), a veterinary charity that was to become another beneficiary of charitable contributions at his funeral.

I functioned on autopilot, my head in three places: work; Sacha; David. David was usually understanding and supportive, but he was also human and would lose his rag from time to time. He worried about me, as did my friends and family. They weren't sure how long I could keep it up, and neither was I. In the final year of Sacha's life, I really came to understand how tough it is for carers of people with mental health issues, and how little support they actually get 'in the community'.

We rowed back toward the jetty. Peering at the shoreline through the binoculars I noticed a couple of grey stone towers in semi-ruins.

'*Chullpas,*' Quizás told me, without my asking. '*Casas antiguas de los muertos.*'

Ancient homes for the dead. I teared up.

Quizás stopped rowing and asked me what was wrong.

'*Nada,*' I retorted.

He looked at me closely. I could feel him reading me. He nodded empathically, then continued rowing.

I blew my nose.

As the coach pulled away from Titicaca, and the highest lake in the world receded from view, I recalled the image of Sacha in my living room, shortly before his death, reclining on the futon behind me while I chanted. Although he was suffering from psychosis at the time, his face looked serene and peaceful. With his hands folded in prayer position under his cheek, he chanted behind me with a barely audible whisper. I glanced back at him. The image of the reclining Sri Lankan Buddha flashed through my mind, and the sense of peace and eternity I'd experienced in its presence flowed through me.

'You look just like the reclining Polonnaruwa Buddha,' I told him.

'Cool,' he replied.

# devils and dust

## rage

My mood was murderous.

About forty kilometres down the road from Titicaca, the coach driver pulled into a nondescript town called Juliaca, parked in the main street and then vanished into thin air. No one dared to get off the coach in case he reappeared and drove away without them. We assumed that he'd gone in search of a more civilised lavatory in which to relieve himself, as the one in the coach was full to overflowing, but after an hour the general consensus amongst the passengers seemed to be that he either had prostate problems or a woman in Juliaca.

The poor hostess, who hadn't a clue where he was either, got some undeserved flak, particularly because she was insistent that she wasn't allowed to serve food while the coach was stationary.

As the young kids on board became increasingly hot, tetchy and restless, their parents dragged them around the coach, pausing to moan to fellow passengers. The only Gringo present, I sympathised politely as they shuffled past, privately relieved that the seat beside me was empty and that I didn't have one of them hissing in my ear that they could happily slice off the driver's *cajones*. After a while most of them drifted back to their seats and, like me, proceeded to stare out the window in a grim, silent funk.

I'd chosen this route because I wanted to see the reputedly breathtaking scenery between Puno and Cusco, but now, even if the driver did bother to reappear, it would be too dark. The travel agent who had booked me into a Cusco hostel had kindly offered to meet me off the coach at 8.30pm and drive me there. I called and told her not to trouble as I had no idea what time I'd be arriving. Sighing, I decided I'd have to face the Cusco bus station touts alone.

Then, a moment of rage. 'It's all *your* fault Sacha,' I hissed to myself. 'If you'd bothered to stay alive I wouldn't be in this absurd, bloody predicament.'

As the minutes ticked by, the mood on the coach evolved from being pissed off into one of passive concern. I listened to the elderly couple behind me, who were convinced no mistress was worth risking such a sought-after job as driving a Royal coach for. They then went on to speculate as to whether our driver had been run over, had a heart attack or been murdered.

I was too irritated to listen to uplifting music and decided that Bruce Springsteen's *Devils and Dust* album more fittingly mirrored my mood. The town was dusty and the driver, I decided, demonic. My iPod had to compete with the robotic throb of banal Spanish pop music thumping its way out of a nearby bar. I persevered. Tracks like 'Long Time Comin'' and 'Matamoros Banks' (about a Mexican immigrant who died en route to his destination) managed to produce something resembling a smirk, until 'Jesus Was An Only Son' – a homage to Mary's relationship with her dying son – came on and flipped me back into Sachaland. Thanks, Bruce.

My relationship with my 'dying son' became, in his final year, a full-on white-knuckle ride, although for a short period of time in the summer of 2004, I was beginning to think that we might have turned a corner.

Sacha had been off methadone for a couple of months and was taking anti-depressants. The flat above his came up for sale, along with the freehold of both properties. Although at the time we couldn't really afford it, David and I decided to buy it anyway. Ostensibly this was because it seemed too good an opportunity to miss but, for my part, I knew that Sacha needed to feel safe with whoever was living above him. Being landlords would give us some measure of control over who lived there.

A couple of pretty, dippy girls who had just finished their degrees at Sussex University became the first tenants. Sacha's tales of life on the road impressed them and they all became friends. He also discovered that an old school friend from London called Mikey, whom he'd once played with in a school band, was living in the same road. Mikey was still playing in bands in Brighton and this opened up possibilities for Sacha.

He and I were having more fun together too. We had some great walks on the Downs with the dogs, and afterwards we'd go out for breakfast or a drink. Sometimes Sacha would knock up a stir-fry for us or a *salade niçoise*, and we'd sit down together and watch a DVD.

My parents hosted a birthday party for me in the summer. They promised Sacha a new guitar if he managed to stay clean, and my elder sister Suzanne, who lives beside a lake in the west of Ireland, promised him a fishing holiday on the same condition. Although he was still missing Rebecca, he seemed much happier. I dared to hope that some kind of heroin-free normality was slowly returning to his life – and mine.

Not long after the party, I spent the weekend with my younger sister Sally. As the evening progressed, I had the feeling she needed to get something off her chest. Sally is a talented and sensitive artist who lived and worked for many years in Africa, where it would appear she picked up the unwelcome intuitive gift of being able to sense a person's approaching death through looking into their eyes. I used to joke that I was thinking of keeping my shades on when I was around her. But it was no joke; the last two people about whom Sally had made this prediction, neither of them old, had indeed died unexpectedly.

Sally was only ten years older than Sacha and looked upon him as a younger brother. The pair had always been close. After a couple of glasses of wine, she announced that, on the evening of my party, she and Sacha had stayed up chatting long after the rest of us had gone to bed, and that she'd seen death in his eyes. In tears, she added, 'But death can also be beautiful.'

My heart froze as I registered her words, then I burst into floods of frightened tears. The next day, I went into total denial; of course Sacha wasn't going to die. I was furious with Sally for daring to even raise the subject. In retrospect, I realise that we were both being prepared, inexplicably, for the seismic shocks to come.

A few days after Sally's revelation, I had a nightmare: I was on an empty sandy beach rushing away in terror from a huge black wave that was thundering close, threatening to engulf me. I clambered up a high, wobbling, rusty lifeguard tower and clung onto the disintegrating seat at the top. My head was barely above the water and I was gasping for breath. I was about to drown in the tsunami. Fear overwhelmed me and I woke up trembling. I was cold and my heart was racing. I had a feeling in my gut that something bad was going to happen.

Ten hours later, as I sat on Sacha's dog-haired sofa in Brighton drinking tea out of a stained mug, he told me that he was back on smack and had spent the previous night in a London police cell.

The coach driver had been gone for almost two hours and I was dying to stretch my legs. I was up too early for My Grandmother's breakfast that morning and hadn't eaten anything since the cheese roll I'd grabbed in Arequipa bus station. The hostess barred my exit. She warned me – as if I hadn't already guessed – that this driver was very unpredictable, and that if I insisted on getting off the coach I had to stay close.

Apart from the rough-looking rowdy bar, all the stalls and shops were closed. It must have been siesta time. A few feet away, a scabby, grey cat was about to leap onto a pair of young ravens as they pecked at a mouldy corn cob in the gutter. I scared the cat away and noticed other corn cob remnants on the ground. On the corner of the street an old woman had a brazier on the go, and a mountain of cobs beside it. Keeping an eye on the coach, I ran over and bought a couple, devoured them instantly, and bought a couple more. Then I risked it and dashed into the bar for a pee and a Pepsi.

Two policemen were standing in the aisle checking people's papers when I climbed back on board the coach. They seemed to take forever with some of the passengers. The old boy sitting behind me tapped me on the shoulder and whispered that they were fishing for bribes. 'Bribes for what?' I whispered back. Anything, he responded: not to report out-of-date or false national identity cards, contraband, cocaine...

Silence descended on the coach when a couple of middle-aged guys seated together were ordered to retrieve their suitcases. Through the window, I watched as the hostess unlocked the hold and the police rifled through their cases. There followed an angry exchange of words with one of the passengers, and although I couldn't see what they'd found, some cash appeared to change hands.

When one of the policemen asked to see my *documento nacional de identidad* I handed him my passport. He waded through it page by page, examining each and every visa stamp and asking dumb questions like what I was doing in Gran Canaria in 2003. Then they both wanted to see my money.

Remembering that Sacha was thrown into a jail in Ecuador after being falsely accused by the police of forging a signature on his own traveller's cheques, I handed mine over with huge reluctance. They returned the cheques without comment and asked to see my cash. I emptied the contents of my purse into my lap. Picking out US dollars, they held the notes up to the light and tugged hard at them, almost to tearing point, testing the strength of the paper. Finally they handed them back to me and moved on to the next passenger.

Once the police had left the coach, the old man told me that forging US dollars in Peru and smuggling them into the States was big business. Well, they found nothing on me.

'The police found a small piece of heroin on me, Mum,' Sacha said, as I sat on his sofa, the dogs licking away my tears. 'They stopped me outside Victoria station... Just after I collected my new passport... I bumped into an old mate... We had a few pints of Guinness together... You know, to celebrate going to Ireland and all that.'

I paced around the living room, shaking with anger. 'Ireland won't be happening now, Sacha. Suzanne made it clear that you couldn't stay with her unless you were clean. Did you score it in London?'

'No, here in Brighton. It was only a small bit to get me through. You wanted me at your party, Mum, and I was paranoid about going to the passport office...'

'Don't blame me!' I screamed.

'I'm not blaming you, Mum,' he whispered hoarsely.

We went to court in early September. Sacha stayed mostly in the smoking room, chatting with a couple of guys who were also due to appear in court that afternoon. On the television in the waiting room, where I paced up and down, too nervous to read, footage of the gun battle between Chechen rebels and Russian security forces was playing over and over again. Beslan schoolchildren, taken hostage, were being massacred.

It was a Friday afternoon and the magistrate, who clearly wanted to leave early, rushed through the cases like wildfire. I asked to be present in court, and was made to feel like a criminal myself as a vulture-faced usher led me to a viewing area behind a bulletproof glass screen. I felt like an extra in a B-movie; part of me couldn't believe that Sacha's life – or, for that matter, my own – had come to this.

The magistrate let him off the possession of heroin charge. I was disappointed about this. I'd hoped he'd be put on a compulsory drugs programme, where he'd have to stay clean or go to prison.

We went to a nearby pub for a 'celebratory' drink before returning home. Sacha disappeared into the gents' for a long time. I rang my sister Sally, who was anxious to know how we'd got on. She'd been reading about a monastery in Thailand that did heroin detoxes, and when Sacha returned to the table I handed him the phone. He sounded enthusiastic; he liked the idea that the monastery was in the mountains. I looked at his eyes. His pupils were virtually non-existent – 'pinned'. He'd been shooting up in the toilet.

The driver re-boarded the coach barely two minutes after the police had departed and, without explanation or apology, pulled out of Juliaca. Coach drivers are clearly the kings of the road in Peru. They do what they want, where they want, when they want. Had his collusive relationship with the cops not been quite so obvious, he'd have needed a police escort to get back behind the wheel and drive to Cusco, so irate were his passengers.

Once we were moving again, the hostess began serving up the meal. The meat looked suspiciously like *cuy* (guinea pig), the national delicacy. Without hesitation, I declined. Although Inca royalty may have feasted on these rodents, and Peruvian shamans past and present diagnose disease in their clients through examining their entrails, I couldn't abide the thought of *looking* at one of these creatures, let alone consuming one. I rummaged around and managed to find half a packet of Polos.

It was clearly the day for ironic titles because, after the meal, they showed the film *The Accidental Tourist*. The additional irony being that Jake, my American ex who worked in Hollywood on a globally famous TV show, had recently bought a house which used to belong to one of the stars of the film. With a rumbling stomach, I found myself wondering why it was that all the men I broke up with then went off and became hideously rich.

For the last forty-five minutes of this marathon journey, I stretched back on the seat, with my head on the rucksack containing Sacha's ashes. After such a turbulent day, I needed to reconnect with my precious cargo and what lay ahead. I recalled how, at my birthday party, when the family were toasting me, Sacha had suddenly declared 'I love you, Mum,' and then run out of the room, overcome with emotion. However much suffering his 'junkie' persona had caused me, it was only one aspect of my son; he was also capable of great sincerity, generosity and deep, deep love.

I closed my eyes and opened up to the welcome visitor that occasionally intervenes to make grieving less unbearable: peace.

Touts galore were still milling around when the coach finally pulled into Cusco bus station, but they weren't as pushy, thank God, as the ones in Nazca. It was well past midnight, and I asked a taxi driver to take me to Incas Dreams hostel.

Until the arrival of the Conquistadors in the 16th century, Cusco was known as Tahuantinsuyo, 'the navel of the world'. It was the epicentre of the Inca Empire, which stretched into Ecuador, Argentina, Bolivia, Chile and Colombia. At least 10 million subjects were governed from this ancient capital. How their fortunes had reversed.

A most disconcerting sight greeted me as we approached the centre of Cusco. Thousands upon thousands of bedraggled Quechua people were wandering the streets or sleeping rough on pavements under ponchos, their children at their sides. Tied to their backs, or at their feet, as they slept were great piles of green vegetation.

I was on the point of questioning the driver about the bundles of vegetation when he stopped the car and asked me if I had the address of the hostel. I didn't, nor its phone number. He then confessed he'd never heard of Incas Dreams. We drove around for ages, stopping to ask passers-by. Eventually, I had no choice but to call the travel agent who had offered to meet me. To my relief, she was still up and explained that the hostel had opened only a couple of weeks earlier. We eventually managed to find the place.

At Incas Dreams, the night porter, whom I'd woken up, couldn't – or perhaps didn't want to – understand why I wasn't thrilled to be given a room which had the communal computer bang outside the door, and windows that looked out into the interior atrium, which was a huge echo chamber. I was too tired to argue, and asked him if there was anything I could eat. It may have been three in the morning but I was famished and still too wired to sleep. He returned with a bowl of dried beans, which I accepted graciously. Not a day for *haute cuisine*.

# jesus dolls

## surviving christmas

At seven the following morning I was woken up by some guy ringing to inform me that he was the breakfast steward, and wanting to know if I was making my way down for breakfast or whether I wanted it in my room. When I opted for the latter, a handsome young man duly appeared with a tray of bread rolls and a pot of tea. He told me his name was Alfredo; he was twenty and studying to be a tour guide.

'My English is so good,' he boasted, 'because my father is an English teacher.'

Alfredo was also rather nosy. Like Victor in Huacachina, he remarked that it was strange to see a woman travelling alone, and wanted to know why. He also wanted to know why I'd slept in the single bed and not in the double. Irritated, I complained that the night porter had told me breakfast would be served until nine and that I didn't like my room.

'It's Christmas Eve; you should be up early,' Alfredo sanctimoniously declared as he poured out my tea. 'And if you don't like the room complain to the manageress, not me.'

So he was bossy, too.

'This is *mate de coca*; tea made from coca leaves,' he informed me as he handed me the cup. 'I've prepared it for you because you've just arrived and it's good for *soroche* – altitude sickness. You don't want to resort, like some tourists in Cusco, to using pills or oxygen.'

'Is there is any cocaine in it?' I asked, wishing he'd made me a double espresso instead of what looked like brownish washing-up water with bits of vegetation floating around in it. He shook his head.

'Not this one. It's been decocainised.'

'That's a shame,' I joked. 'I could do with a lift after being woken up so early.'

Alfredo's face broke into a smile, at last, and he apologised for the early breakfast, explaining that he had to attend Mass at the university.

'Before you go, Alfredo, can you tell me why there are thousands of Indigenous people camped out in the centre of Cusco?'

'Every year they walk long distances from the countryside to sell their mosses and grasses for our nativity displays at the Christmas Eve market in La Plaza de Armas,' he explained. 'You must not miss it.'

As much as I admired Incas Dreams' tasteful renovation

163

and décor, I made it clear to Maria, the manageress who was reluctant to relocate me, that if she didn't I was checking out. It worked and I was given a lovely room complete with a queen bed and balcony which looked out onto a delightful narrow, cobbled street. Perfect. I reserved a similar room for Roberto and left a message with his sister in Bogotá, where he was due to arrive in a few days' time before flying on to meet me here.

At the end of the call I was suddenly gripped with anxiety about Roberto's arrival. His behaviour was so unpredictable. What was I letting myself in for? But it was too late now to change anything.

Still half asleep and with *soroche* kicking in despite the coca tea, I made my way to the market. Every building I passed, from homes and hotels to petrol stations and designer shops, either had a nativity scene on display or was in the process of constructing one.

In La Plaza de Armas, the Christmas Eve market was already in full swing. The Quechua had made this enormous space their own, rendering it impossible to walk on the pavements or drive up the streets. Little children were tied with bundles of rags to their mothers' backs; dirty clothes, filthy faces, shoeless feet; the stench of urine everywhere. In their colourfully patterned Andean ponchos and *ruanas* (large alpaca shawls), the Indigenous people resembled a bizarre football crowd, camped out on a pitch.

I wove my way through a mass of makeshift, ground-level stalls, displaying moss, greenery, saplings, straw, ready-made nativity scenes, candles, incense and herbs.

The high-pitched haggling was deafening.

The sombre, fortress-like cathedral which overlooked the plaza appeared uninviting, but promised a temporary refuge from the overwhelming crowd. Once inside, I was startled by its lush, gleaming interior and gawped at altars made entirely from beaten, embossed silver; a solid gold crucifix covered in precious gemstones; and exquisite Renaissance paintings. Dotted here and there were life-sized Jesus mannequins. Prim velvet skirts or what resembled 1980s Marks & Spencer petticoats delicately concealed Our Lord's privates.

But I couldn't stop yawning. As an altitude daze took over, Cusco cathedral appeared more and more lavish and Disney-like. I sat down inside the Chapel El Señor de los Temblores (Chapel of the Lord of the Earthquakes) where a huge canvas hung on the wall, depicting the massive earthquake that had hit the city in 1650, and attempted to process the cathedral's sensory overload.

This 16th-century edifice had been constructed on the site of the Inca Viracocha's demolished palace. And as much as I loved its interior, I also found the intricate, lavish gold and silver work, the wooden carvings, the artistry and overall beauty, a little difficult to reconcile with the abject, heaving throng of poverty-stricken Indigenous people congregated in the plaza outside. It had, ironically, been the Quechans' forebears who had created most of the cathedral's ornate beauty. In an act of defiance, the native craftsmen had carved a puma head on the main door. I liked that.

The sky was overcast and the air moist as I left the

cathedral and wove my way back through the bewildering Quechan market. Fascinating as it all was, I was hyperconscious of being a comparatively rich person, and felt guilty having to say '*no, gracias*' over and over again. Against my better judgement, I paid a little Quechan lad generously for a lump of moss, and was immediately swamped by other kids wanting to sell me more of the same.

I attempted to speed-walk through the plaza but a hungry-eyed woman playing *zampoña* panpipes grabbed the sleeve of my anorak. In a flash I remembered how Sacha had needed to busk in the centre of Brighton last Christmas Eve, and impulsively handed her my few remaining sol.


Sacha was busking for the cash to buy presents – which made a welcome change from busking to buy heroin. Since the court case, I'd been trying my hardest to get him back onto a drugs programme and, once again, it was a long, difficult process, involving endless appointments for referrals. All of which, again, meant pushing, pushing and pushing – something which addicts without pushy relatives like me find nearly impossible, whereas scoring smack is incredibly easy.

Until he was accepted on a new programme, Sacha still needed heroin to feed his habit and also the money to buy it. The praise he received from strangers for his harmonica playing, being able to pay his own way and pay back my loans to him, improved his self-esteem and I encouraged him to busk. I'd long ago given up caring what other people thought. All that mattered now was his recovery and survival. So what if people questioned why this middle-class, middle-aged professional's son was a busker? I'd rather that than he was stealing from the poor or blowing people's heads off for a living.

Sometimes though, he wasn't able to earn enough. One morning he called me very early and begged me to put some money into his bank account; he was becoming sick and needed to score. He promised he'd pay me back. I knew that he was desperate, because Sacha only ever contacted me for money when all else had failed. After I'd paid a visit to a branch of his bank, I called him.

'You saved my life Mum,' he said. 'You saved my life.'

I felt a rush of adrenaline, followed by immense relief and sadness. This wasn't how I wanted to save his life. All I'd saved him from was the agony of going cold turkey.

Only in the run-up to Christmas, after he'd accidentally swallowed a bag of heroin he was hiding in his mouth – which could have been fatal – was he finally fast-tracked onto another drug programme. This time he was given Subutex, the superior heroin substitute. His new drug team were supportive, he had a good key worker, and he agreed, finally, to have counselling when a slot became available.

But just as Sacha was getting back on track, David needed emergency surgery for an infected gall bladder. At the time he was working as a freelance cameraman and editor. Some years earlier he'd had a serious motorbike accident that had kept him off work for six months – every freelancer's nightmare. We dreaded this happening again.

Sacha relished the opportunity to show concern for David and to support me. He'd been partly responsible for the fact that I'd been, by this time, married to David for nine years; the first guy I'd dated since the breakup of my second marriage who had actually met with Sacha's approval. After meeting David for the first time Sacha said, 'He's real, Mum, he's real,' and encouraged me to pursue the relationship. They bonded over a shared love of dogs, music and an interest in the Traveller movement. David's best friend was also 'on the road'. To our relief, David recovered from his operation surprisingly quickly – and in time for Christmas.

Back at Incas Dreams, I queued up to check my email on the communal computer. There was one from David, now several days old, telling me that an art gallery had approached him about putting on a solo exhibition of his photography. Over the years he'd made a living in a variety of different ways: policeman; professional golfer; aerial photographer; documentary filmmaker; but his real love had always been photography. I was so happy for him.

Rather than have a gripe-fest, I thought I'd tell him what had made me laugh that day: after leaving the Chapel El Señor de los Temblores in the cathedral, my eyes had alighted upon a large oil painting, *The Last Supper*, by one Marcos Zapata; I was unable to suppress an irreverent giggle. The disciples sat around, as usual, revering the central figure of Christ. Laid out sacrificially on the table before him, with its little feet sticking up in the air, was a *cuy*. For his last supper, Jesus Christ was about to enjoy the Andean feast of roast guinea pig. And why not?

Christmas Day. I was on the phone to my parents in England, trying my hardest not to sound too lonely and sober. They were in a predictably pissed, Christmassy mood, but it was still only eight in the morning in Peru. To my surprise, a tearful-sounding David, who had dropped by to see them, came on the line. I felt a spasm of guilt as I acknowledged, once again, how difficult this solitary journey of mine must be for him. He hadn't asked for any of this. Was it fair on him to have come away at all – especially over Christmas? No.

Rather than mope around in my room, I made a beeline for the centre of Cusco, exchanging a *'Feliz Navidad'* and a smile with just about everyone en route. A lively procession of dancing Quechans decked out in feathers and woollen *ukuku* (trickster) masks was weaving its way along the Avenida Sol to the clamorous accompaniment of Andean instruments.

Not far behind it was a slow, sombre procession. Kitted out in white robes were men carrying aloft icons and statues of the Virgin and child. I grabbed my camera, excited at snapping the most arresting and significantly juxtaposed images of Quechan and Spanish culture I'd encountered so far, but the damn thing wouldn't work.

As I wandered around, looking for a camera repair shop that might be open on Christmas Day, I couldn't help noticing that a disproportionate number of women appeared to be carrying a baby, wrapped in a white shawl. I managed to find a shop and handed over the camera. Once I was outside again, lo and behold, vast numbers of women of varying ages, shapes and sizes – families in tow – were now carrying not babies, but dolls of varying ages, shapes and sizes, swaddled in lace and finery. I followed them into a church, which was almost full to overflowing with people.

Inside the church I saw that the dolls they were cradling and those on display were more reminiscent of the ones I'd played with as a child than modern-day Barbies. Each woman in the congregation slowly approached the altar and held out her doll to be blessed by the priest. Trestle tables laden with dolls lined the walls of the church. Presumably they belonged to absent, or even deceased, members of the congregation, as some of the dolls looked distinctly ancient.

I was fascinated to think that each family had its very own treasured baby Jesus doll, which was taken out of the cupboard once a year along with the decorations, scrubbed down, polished and then blessed by the priest on Christmas morning. Sadly, this lovely tradition left me feeling bereft. I hungered for one too, but a real one, a real grown-up one, a real grown-up one called Sacha, not Jesus.

Last Christmas Sacha was concerned that his old school friend, Mikey, who had not only broken up with his girlfriend but had broken his leg too, would be spending Christmas on his own, and asked if he could join us. I drove down to Brighton on Christmas morning to pick them both up. Dressed in his best trousers and smartest hoodie, Sacha answered the door, smiling happily.

'I've had a bath Mum,' he reassured me, as he climbed into the car with the dogs and his black dustbin bag full of presents and wrapping paper.

It was a relief not to have to remind him to have a bath. Now he was back on his feet again and able to take responsibility for himself once more. For the three years that I'd been helping out with his clucks, and, more recently, as his designated carer, our relationship had, inevitably, reverted at times to that of parent/child. Something neither of us relished. Nevertheless, as we drew up outside Mikey's flat, he laughed like a kid and said, 'I'm so excited!' Unlike his mother, Sacha still loved the paraphernalia of Christmas.

I'd been warned that the first Christmas without him wouldn't be easy, but I decided, for Sacha's sake, to celebrate as best I could. I found a restaurant overlooking the almost-empty Plaza de Armas, ordered a Pisco Sour and asked for the menu.

From the restaurant window I watched the few remaining

Quechans doggedly trying to sell their wares to disinterested passers-by. The plaza was once the ancient Inca ceremonial centre of Huacapata; I found it sad that after a 24-hour sojourn in their ancestral home these Indigenous people had to pack up, yet again, and head for the countryside. I contemplated the menu. At the table next to mine a noisy, vivacious family, its members ranging from around nine months to ninety, were busy exchanging gifts.

Last Christmas, along with *Lost Treasures of the World,* Sacha had given me a beautiful green glass vase. My son was very giving, and many of his diverse gifts graced the shelves, walls, window ledges and floors of our home – a UFO lamp, a painted Chinese plate, an ornamental swan, a wrought-iron mirror, a heart-shaped sandstone pot containing bath oils, a palm, a yucca, a bamboo, a green trailing plant inside a huge goldfish bowl…

I glanced down at the silver ring on my finger he'd given me for Christmas when he was sixteen. He'd bought it from a jeweller's shop in South Kensington, next to Condomania: the first-ever condom shop in England where, despite endless teasing, he'd managed to hold down a Saturday job. I started to weep as it dawned on me that I'd never receive another gift from him. Those I now had were destined to become my treasures.

The waitress finally appeared to take my order. The family on the next table were getting rowdier, and I didn't have much of an appetite. I hesitated; then asked for a Peruvian chicken dish with chilli called *Aji de Gallina,* and a *Cusqueña* beer.

Sacha had insisted on all the trimmings last Christmas: bread sauce, cranberry jelly and stuffing, and ample supplies of tequila for himself and Shiraz for Mikey. I bought Dodge and Ruff Christmas stockings containing doggy sweets and squeaky Santa-head toys that drove us all crazy. We pulled the crackers and lit the incense burner Sacha had bought David. The atmosphere was cosy, fun and loving.

After the meal, David drifted off upstairs and the three of us continued to drink, joke and reminisce into the night. Mikey talked about rifts with his family, and how he'd fallen out with his mother, who claimed to be a white witch and had moved to Spain.

'Sacha loves you so much,' Mikey said.

'I don't know what I would have done without her over the last couple of years,' my son added. Then he asked to hear some of my favourite music, a request he'd never made before, so we listened to Handel's *Messiah* and the alternative rock band, Placebo.

He and Mikey had agreed they'd make music together in the coming year, and chatted excitedly about their plans. Sacha was also keen to get Headflux up and running again. Aware that one day he would inherit quite a bit of money from his father, Sacha talked about how he could build care homes for street kids in South America. I promised him that if he stayed clean, I would pay for him to visit Roberto in Africa in January.

I paid up pronto and left the restaurant; these recollections were heart-searing and I had to keep on the move. The wizard who had managed to fix my camera told me the sensor had gone because there was sand inside it. So my grand Huacachina dune ascent had come at a price.

Back in my room at Incas Dreams a tinny, synthesised version of 'Silent Night', one of my favourite carols, started up out of nowhere. Worse was to come. The moment it finished, 'Jingle Bells' began, and then back to 'Silent Night' again, ad infinitum. I eventually traced the sickly sound to speakers attached to a string of fat fairy lights strung above my balcony. I didn't think another complaint would go down too well with Maria, so I switched the satellite television on at full volume.

'Christ! How sad is this!' I muttered to myself, as I lay on the bed watching, for the first time in my life, the Queen's speech. She talked about how humanity had suffered during the past year: the tsunami, Hurricane Katrina in New Orleans, the earthquake in Pakistan, the 7/7 London bombings. But she didn't mention Iraq, rendition, Guantanamo Bay or, for that matter, my Sacha.

Hauling myself out of bed, I removed my ear plugs and groaned. 'Jingle Bells' was still gnawing away in the background and overnight I'd mysteriously acquired a streaming cold. I'd love to have spent Boxing Day in bed but I'd been advised to buy my train tickets to Machu Picchu as soon as possible as there was only one train a day and a great number of tourists at this time of year.

I made my way down the atrium stairs, recalling how, last Boxing Day morning, Sacha was in the middle of vacuuming the living room when David and I went downstairs for breakfast. David had switched on the television and images of the tsunami that had just struck South East Asia flashed across the screen. We picked at our breakfast in silent shock. One of the coastal resorts in Sri Lanka, where we'd stayed exactly a year earlier, had been devastated. All the local people we'd befriended would, more than likely, have drowned. A year earlier it would have been us. How fragile and random life suddenly seemed.

Cusco station booking office was incredibly busy, with numbered waiting billets for the ticket desks. I began wondering, as I twiddled my thumbs while waiting for my number to come up, whether Sacha had sat in this same ticket office. Then I remembered that he'd started the Inca Trail in the Sacred Valley. Perhaps he took the train back to Lima from here after seeing Machu Picchu? Perhaps he flew back? I'd never know because I couldn't ask him.

An impassioned rant kicked off in my head.

'Why can't we spend Christmas together again? Why have you made me a childless mother at this time of nativity? Why did you have to die? I tried everything I could to keep you alive. Every door was slammed in my face. I gave up my home, and my time, to endless, useless clucks because you refused to go into rehab. I got you onto numerous drug programmes and begged you to go for counselling. I re-mortgaged my home to buy you a flat, to provide you with some stability. The pain and anxiety I felt, when I was unable to contact you and had no idea where you were, was the stuff of nightmares. Oh Sacha! Sacha! What hell you've put me through.'

Elisabeth Kübler-Ross, the late Swiss humanist psychiatrist and expert on dying, death and grief, claimed that the bereaved flip-flop in and out of different stages of grief: denial; anger; bargaining; depression; acceptance. I knew for sure which one I was in then. According to Kübler-Ross, the bereaved could find themselves in a rage about the deceased's 'negligent' doctor, someone who failed to turn up at the funeral or – more to the point for me on that Boxing Day – the beloved who had abandoned them. Anger, she maintained, was an essential part of the healing process, because it provided a temporary structure to the nothingness of loss.

My number came up and I put the diatribe on hold. I bought two 'backpacker' tickets to Machu Picchu for myself and Sacha's father on 30th December. I walked away from the station in a tsunami of tears; Kübler-Ross had also said that lurking beneath bereavement anger was pain. I realised that I was trying to block out the memory of Boxing Day the year before because it was simply too painful.

We'd been invited for drinks at my brother Neil's, where my parents were also spending Christmas. They hadn't seen Sacha for a while, and everyone hugged him and warmly welcomed Mikey as he limped in on his crutches.

The canapés soon appeared, along with champagne. David took photos of Sacha unawares. He hated having his picture taken. In the pictures, he looks shy, but smiley and incredibly happy. Still with a beard, he hadn't yet used my Christmas present of a razor and beard trimmer. Sister Sally rang and had a long chat with him. I recall my mother whispering in his ear: 'How's my boy then? We love you, Sacha.'

Mikey, Sacha and his two young cousins Alex and Laurence started making music. Thinking that everyone was laughing at him when we were simply smiling in appreciation, the sensitive young Laurence stood up to sing and then ran out of the room. Sacha followed him out and comforted him. When he returned, Sacha began playing his harmonica, and we all listened in rapt silence. Everyone there, with the exception of his young cousins, knew what Sacha had been/was going through. My father and David were clearly moved as Sacha did a solo rendering of the blues. Both had struggled with attempting to master the harmonica and admitted to being envious of Sacha's talent.

Later, back home, David told him that he really should become a session musician. And those were his last words to Sacha.

Months afterwards, my father remarked how happy and serene Sacha had appeared that afternoon. It's true. He was, on reflection, in a kind of altered state. There was a total calm about him; he glowed. As Shakespeare's Romeo remarked: 'How oft when men are at the point of death have they been merry! Their keepers call it lightning before death.'

A year later in a country far away, gratitude welled up inside me as I acknowledged that the previous Christmas and Boxing Day had, in fact, bequeathed some cherished memories. Sacha had turned to me, on the A23 as I was driving him and Mikey back to Brighton, and thanked me profusely.

'That, Mum, was the best Christmas I've had for years.'

# the sacred valley

### solstice solace

I stood on a corner of La Plaza de Armas waiting for a coach to pick me up for a tour of the Sacred Valley. Already, it was an hour late and I was growing impatient. I wanted to visit this sacred area of temples and citadels because I was keen to understand more about Inca civilisation in readiness for my trip to Machu Picchu.

The Nazca and the Inca were separate civilisations. The Incas had no written language, and therefore no recorded history. Apart from archaeological findings, the main source of information about them seemed to come from a confessional preamble in the will, written in 1589, of the last of the Conquistadors, Don Mancio Serra de Leguisamo. He declared himself guilty because he and his fellow Conquistadors had 'destroyed by our evil example, the people who had such a government as was enjoyed by these natives'.

I'd made the booking at a Cusco tour agency on Christmas Day with a sleepy, hungover-looking guy called Nico, who had clearly drawn the short straw by having to work. I later noticed that the receipt he handed me looked very unconvincing, and recalled that he hadn't even taken down my name. I returned the next day and was issued with a proper ticket by a guy called Victor, who must have been Nico's identical twin.

When I walked into the agency on the appointed day I was met not by Nico or Victor, but this time by Ernesto. Either they were triplets, or I was starting to lose the plot. In between bouts of running around the plaza like a headless chicken in search of the coach, Ernesto was trying his hardest to reassure me that the Sacred Valley tour was definitely on.

But the omens weren't good.

My day had got off to a pretty *un*sacred start after I'd managed to break the cistern in my en-suite WC in the early hours of the morning, resulting in a gushing, waterfall-like din echoing throughout the entire hostel and waking everyone up. I'd just managed to get back to sleep and was having a wonderful dream involving Sacha and birds when the night porter rang to ask if my toilet was broken. I responded in the affirmative; he said he hadn't a clue how to fix it.

I'd woken up, again, an hour or two later, to 'Jingle Bells' and a dangerously dipping mood. What to do? Enlightenment came with the realisation that I had to put a stop to those crappy carols before I leaped off the balcony.

I strode into the hostel office and told Maria that the noise was making me *completamente loca* (completely crazy). She insisted there was absolutely nothing she could do about the offending décor because the guy who had strung it up there was off work for a week.

Still fuming, I stormed into the breakfast bar. Alfredo, the student who manned it, asked me what was up, so I told him. He walked over to a cupboard, opened the door and pulled out a plug. Sorted. Except Maria was now in a bad mood.

'You won't lose your job, will you?' I whispered over the counter.

'Don't worry,' Alfredo replied, with a broad grin. 'My auntie owns this place.'

The coach finally arrived and parked on the other side of the plaza. I rushed over and clambered aboard. Once inside, I was disconcerted to discover that this long-awaited vehicle was bursting at the seams with hot, fed-up-looking people of various nationalities who had been slowly collected from hotels and hostels all over Cusco – a luxury denied to me, as the street outside my hostel was too narrow for a coach to get down. The last to board, I had to squeeze in beside a tense, morbidly obese Venezuelan bloke. This was going to be fun.

The coach stopped on the outskirts of Cusco to pick up the Quechua guide, a tall, dark, wiry guy in his thirties, who was full of nervous energy and fluent in English. I was the only native English speaker on board, and he encouraged me to ask him as many questions as I liked.

Ten minutes later, the coach stopped off at a market so that we could all spend lots of money and the driver could get his tip from the stallholders. Five minutes after that, it stopped again, this time to take in a llama farm. As much as I admired these bizarre, loveable creatures, I found myself wondering if we were ever going to make it to El Valle Sagrado.

Once everyone had finished taking photos, we boarded the coach once more and finally headed for the valley. Before long, a steep, viridescent valley, stretching high above the gushing Vilcanota-Urubamba River, came into view. The river eventually snaked its way out into an alluvial, fertile plain, which was home to several microclimates, Inca sites and little market towns. The main attractions in the valley, the guide informed us, were the lofty Inca citadels of Pisac and Ollantaytambo: the taking-off point for the Inca Trail leading to Machu Picchu.

I'd been expecting a bit of a climb at Pisac, but this was a two-hour hike. No laughing matter in such high altitude. Thankfully, I wasn't the only flagger in the group. My corpulent coach-mate didn't set foot outside the bus.

Halfway up the climb, I was moved by the sight of a little Quechua boy playing an Andean flute. I handed him a few coins and sat down on a nearby rock to take a breather. In the distance, I could see someone paragliding down the valley. I vaguely remembered Sacha recounting a story of how he'd waited hours for a turn at paragliding across a valley when travelling in Peru. The punters had been impatiently jostling to be the next in the queue. He stood back, allowing them all to go before him, and was rewarded for his patience by being flown all around the valley for twice as long as everyone else. Could it have been here, I wondered?

We eventually reached a high plateau; below it lay a deep gorge and a lush green vista stretching as far as the eye could see. Peppered with ruins of temples and tombs, the agricultural terracing and drainage below the ancient site had been constructed centuries ago by the Incas who first farmed this fertile land. The fact it was still in use was a testament to the inventiveness, community and orderliness that so characterised the Inca Empire.

The Conquistador with a guilty conscience claimed that he and his compatriots had: '…found these kingdoms in such good order, and the said Incas governed them in such ways that throughout them there was not a thief, nor a vicious man, nor an adulteress, nor were there immoral people. The men had honest and useful occupations. The lands, forests, mines, pastures, houses and all kinds of products were regulated and distributed in such sort that each one knew his property.'

The guide walked over to me and pointed out an Andean condor flying overhead. The sight of this magnificent creature brought back the dream I'd had the night before. I was standing in London's Victoria station feeling anxious. Sacha had gone to the chemist to buy some medicine, and I'd lost sight of him in the crowd. When he eventually returned, my sense of relief was overwhelming. We hugged and hugged and hugged.

'What do you do now?' my dream-self asked Sacha.

'I look after the birds,' he replied.

Then I was transported to my patio at home, where I gazed at the bluetits that nest there every year. Out of nowhere, hundreds of other birds appeared, along with friendly dogs and puppies which licked me all over. Sacha stood beside me, giggling. I was gloriously happy. Until I woke up.

As I watched the condor swoop across the Sacred Valley, I couldn't help wondering if there was something rather mystic about our feathered friends and the characteristics they display, some so fierce and others so gentle: vultures, doves, and all the thousands of species on the spectrum between them. Perhaps they were even reincarnated souls?

Since arriving in Peru I'd read *Man's Search for Meaning* – the Austrian psychiatrist Viktor Frankl's heart-rending account of life in the concentration camps. Frankl describes how, labouring away one day to dig a trench in the snow, sick to death of insults and abuse from the guards, he began communing in his mind with his beloved wife. He did not, at that time, know whether she was dead or alive. Suddenly, he sensed her presence, and the feeling was so powerful that he felt he could almost reach out and grasp her. At that very moment, a bird flew down, perched right in front of him on a heap of soil he'd just dug, and stared up at him steadily. Only later did he discover that by that time his wife had, in fact, already perished in the Holocaust. This incident later led Frankl to conclude: 'Love goes very far beyond the physical presence of the beloved ... Love is as strong as death.'

Once back on the coach, we drove a few kilometres from Pisac, pulled up outside a large hacienda and trooped in for a buffet lunch. I was so busy making sure I didn't eat guinea pig that I managed to miss out on the fresh trout. I tried, without success, to make conversation with a surly young Danish couple who looked as if they'd just had a row, and wished I'd sat at a Spanish-speaking table instead. It was a relief when the guide blew his whistle, summoning us back onto the coach. Our next stop, he informed us, was the Inca tribute gathering and administrative centre of Ollantaytambo, some 2,800 metres above sea level.

Laid out as a grid system by the Incas, this delightful little town was full of artisan stalls, their female owners dressed in the local costume of patterned *manta* shawls and black-and-red woven skirts and hats. Ollantaytambo was resplendent with flowers. Even the entrance of the 17th-century church of Santiago Apóstolo, with its Inca-style stone belfry and enormous bells, had flowers painted all over it.

Overshadowing Ollantaytambo was a massive temple-fortress, which the Incas had constructed on a steep mountainside. The temple-fortress was foreboding, yet more impressive than the ruins at Pisac. But my heart sank as I realised this meant another climb.

Thousands of Incas must have slaved away, transporting the huge blocks of stone that had been quarried from a mountainside six kilometres away. Then they had to haul them up the mountainside. All I had to carry was a small rucksack. The Incas had a strict work ethic. No one went hungry in the Inca Empire, but laziness wasn't tolerated. The guide pointed to a prison they'd built, halfway up an almost vertical slope nearby, for those who skived off work. Not that I blamed them.

If Don Mancio is to be believed, laziness was about the only crime for which an Inca was ever banged up: 'They were so free from the committal of crimes or excesses, men as well as women, that the Indian who had 100,000 pesos' worth of gold or silver in his house left it open, merely placing a small stick against the door, as a sign that its master was out. When they saw that we put locks and keys on our doors and found that we had thieves among us, and men who sought to make their daughters commit sin, they despised us.'

Staring out over the Urubamba Valley, I was beginning to understand what an incredible people the Incas were, and why their civilisation had so fascinated my son. He would have started his five-day Inca Trail hike to Machu Picchu just a short distance from here. Originally the sacred, hidden track that Inca royalty took to Machu Picchu, the trail was now a trekkers' pilgrimage route, winding its way along stretches of the Andes and through the tropical forests of the Amazon Basin.

On the coach journey back to Cusco I bombarded the guide with questions about the Incas. He suggested I paid a visit to the Inca temple of Koricancha while I was in Cusco, and that I read the American explorer Hiram Bingham's *Lost City of the Incas*. I had a copy in my suitcase which I hadn't yet opened. It was still daylight when the coach pulled into Cusco and I made a beeline for Koricancha.

*Koric* means 'golden enclosure', and the temple was once tastefully embellished with gold. Sadly, all the gold was stripped away to fill Atahualpa's ransom room. This sumptuous temple, which was also an observatory, once housed 4,000 priests and their followers; now it was a hybrid of Inca and colonial architecture.

Juan Pizarro, brother of the more famous Francisco, had generously bequeathed Koricancha to the Dominicans, who proceeded to construct an uninspiring, baroque church alongside the temple, which they named Santo Domingo. In the distance I could see monks flitting around in brown cassocks.

Inside the temple I discovered that the Incas had worshipped a huge, golden sun-shaped disc, known as a *punchau*. During the summer solstice, the sun's rays shone directly into a tabernacle-like niche in which the Inca in power at the time sat. Known as the Sapa Inca, he was believed to be the son of the sun god Inti, and, therefore, immortal. Mummies of dead Incas were brought out, dusted down (much like, I imagined, the Jesus dolls I'd seen on Christmas Day), propped up against the walls of the temple and treated as important guests at solstice sun-worshipping ceremonies. I closed my eyes and tried to picture an Inca solstice celebration, but a powerful memory surfaced instead.

It was June 2001. David and I were heading to Devizes for a weekend away in our VW camper when we noticed a long line of traffic going into Stonehenge.

We went to investigate and ended up in a field nearby, with other campers and Travellers who told us that Stonehenge was about to be opened to the public for the summer solstice for the first time in many years. Until then we hadn't even clocked that it was the solstice. The field was filling up with crusties and New Agers. Might Sacha be coming down for this? I called him; sure enough, he and Rebecca were intending to set off from London at midnight with a group of friends.

David and I sat around in the early evening, watching stilt walkers, jugglers and other performers putting on ad hoc shows outside their vehicles. We went to bed early, setting our alarm for 3am. Still half asleep, we trudged down to the stones, along with hundreds of others and met up with Sacha and Rebecca. The party was already in full swing.

As the sun came up, we sipped wine and laughed together, our moods elevated by the vibrant atmosphere and head-spinning drumming. I'd witnessed a total eclipse a year or two earlier, when even the seagulls were cowed into silence. The solstice at Stonehenge had a similar intensity, both primal and mystic. We shared a sense of awe as nature took over. The sun, when it rose, was humbling; the light dense and unusual. David took a haunting photograph of Sacha: the phosphorescent sun rising behind him and the ancient stones, his face almost in darkness.

Darkness had descended and there was a chill in the air but I didn't feel like moving from Koricancha. The temple was holding me there. I stroked its walls. The stones weren't held in place with mortar, yet they slotted effortlessly together and had withstood Cusco's seismic tremors. Peru is home to the first stone pyramids, and Inca masonry, like that of the Egyptian pyramids, bordered on the perfect. I sat on the cold stones, deep in thought: these two ancient civilisations had masonry, sun worship and death rituals in common.

I'd always associated mummies and sarcophagi with darkness, damp, death and misery, until, on my fortieth birthday, I'd experienced an epiphany of sorts while visiting the Cairo antiquities museum, which houses the most wonderful collection of ancient Egyptian artefacts. Some of the sarcophagi and gigantic carved statues of pharaohs held lotus flowers in their palms, which the Egyptians considered to be a symbol of creation and rebirth.

The Buddhism I practise is based on the Lotus Sutra; I was fascinated to discover how universal the lotus is in sanctifying the mysterious passage between life, death and rebirth. I gazed up at their serene smiling faces and felt wonderfully uplifted.

Later in the day, after visiting the great pyramid in Giza, as a birthday present to myself I splashed out on some very expensive Egyptian lotus oil. Almost a year ago I'd had to ask David to pour, in the snail-like pattern of the eternity spiral, my Egyptian lotus oil on Sacha's forehead when he was lying in his coffin in the funeral chapel. My own hand was trembling too much.

The ambience in that chapel was sacred, even though his body was sealed in a bag like a mummy – the usual precaution against HIV and hepatitis B and C when handling the body of a junkie, even though Sacha had none of those afflictions. Even in death, my son was being denied the human dignity so many addicts are denied in life.

All human beings, according to the Lotus Sutra, possess the pure life-state of Buddhahood, and for me at least, my lotus-oil death ritual reinforced this. Sacha had made his own connection with the Lotus Sutra and the eternity of life. During his travails, I'd often try to get him to chant with me, but to no avail. He said he'd only practise if and when he was ready. One day, he came down from London, calm and relaxed, and announced he was now ready to chant with us. He did a perfect Gongyo (recitation of small portions of the Lotus Sutra in ancient Chinese and Sanskrit). Sacha believed in the eternity of life.

On that same trip to Egypt, I bought Sacha an *ankh*, the looped cross which is the Egyptian symbol of eternity. The gods were often portrayed holding an *ankh* to someone's lips, offering them the breath of life they would need in the afterlife.

A couple of months after Sacha's death, I went down to Brighton to arrange to sell his flat. We'd already had his furniture cleared out, but for some unknown reason, one piece still remained: an old desk. I opened the drawer of the desk and inside it was the Egyptian *ankh*.

Back at Incas Dreams I rummaged around in my suitcase and found Bingham's *Lost City of the Incas*. It was already past midnight when I crept down to the deserted lobby and started to read about this American who had stumbled upon Machu Picchu in 1911 and considered the Incas to be 'the wisest rulers America had ever seen'. In a matter of minutes I was riveted.

According to Che Guevara, who had also visited the citadel, 'Machu Picchu was to Hiram Bingham the crowning of all his purest dreams as an adult child'. I liked the 'adult child' bit, but I'd developed conflicting feelings about Che, whom I once venerated. I no longer agreed with his belief in violent revolution.

Bingham gave a graphic description of the cruelty meted out to the last Inca. The young Túpac Amaru and his entourage were captured by the Spanish and brought to Cusco in 1572. Bingham described how the viceroy Francisco de Toledo took great pleasure in laying on the spectacle of a mock trial, on the trumped up charge of murdering a Spanish friar. After the trial, captured Inca chiefs were tortured to death with, according to Bingham, 'fiendish brutality', and Túpac Amaru's wife was mangled before his eyes. His own head was cut off and placed on a pole. Túpac's young sons, the last of the Inca line, perished soon afterwards.

All this carnage had apparently taken place on a black scaffold erected outside the cathedral in the Plaza de

Armas; directly opposite the restaurant where I'd been eating my Yuletide lunch. I was grateful not to have known this while I was chomping away on my Christmas chicken.

Our dozy night porter's snores reverberated around the lobby. I didn't want to put the book down so I returned to my room, dragged a lamp out onto the 'Jingle Bells'-free balcony, and continued reading into the early hours of the morning.

Bingham described how, according to eyewitnesses, when Túpac was executed, a multitude of his subjects filled the square, making the skies reverberate with their cries and wailing. Túpac Amaru's last words were: *'Ccollanan Pachacamac ricuy auccaunac yahuarniy hichascancuta.'*

'Mother Earth witness how my enemies shed my blood.'

Toledo, I decided, was a nasty, twisted little brute, who had ruled Peru with an iron fist and a hard heart. He wrote a large volume of laws including: 'Any Indian who makes friendship with an Indian woman who is an infidel, is to receive one hundred lashes, for the first offence... Indians shall no longer use surnames taken from the moon, birds, animals, serpents, or rivers, which they formerly used.'

I grabbed a Kleenex. I couldn't help shedding a tear over the Conquistadors' primitive destruction of what had been – in my opinion – a more balanced, poetic, gentle civilisation which revered Mother Earth. But I was relieved to read that not all the Spanish approved of Toledo's actions. A bishop and several priests, believing the Inca to be innocent, had, on their knees, implored the viceroy not to execute him, but to send him to Spain to be tried by King Philip II. It later transpired that Philip greatly disapproved of the execution of Túpac Amaru.

The 13th-century Japanese Buddhist priest Nichiren Daishonin gave the following advice to one of his followers: 'More valuable than treasures in a storehouse are the treasures of the body, and the treasures of the heart are the most valuable of all.'

Pizarro and Toledo might have accumulated treasures of the storehouse, but only at the expense of treasures of the heart. Still, what goes around comes around. Toledo was later blamed, apparently unfairly, when the viceregal account books failed to balance. He was recalled to Spain in 1581 and sent to prison, where he died three years later. For all his stolen treasure, Pizarro didn't have a very happy ending either. In 1541, he was assassinated, and, sadly, 426 years later, so was Che.

I closed the book and looked up at the silent, star-studded sky, thankful that the day had ended on a more sacred note and that my son had possessed, in abundance, treasures of the heart. I wondered, too, whether El Valle Sagrado was a dress rehearsal for Machu Picchu.

# two hundred coca leaves

## a moving encounter

There was still no sign of Roberto. I'd had enough of sightseeing and was ready to move on from Cusco, but each time I tried to call Bogotá to ascertain his whereabouts, the telephone lines were busy. It occurred to me, as I lay in bed one morning feeling bored, that perhaps my new Incas Dreams friend Alfredo might know the whereabouts of a witch I could interview for this book I was meant to be co-writing.

I wasn't in the best of moods when I sat down at the breakfast bar. Then, as Alfredo handed me my second *café con leche*, he asked me if I'd been crying. Yes, I'd recently had a little weep, but I insisted that my eyes were red because of my cold.

Suddenly, I felt apprehensive about all the personal questions a visit to a witch might trigger, and nearly abandoned my plan. But in the end I swallowed my misgivings and asked him straight out if he could find me a witch. I didn't trust my Spanish enough, I explained, to conduct an accurate interview with someone speaking in the local dialect; his English was so good he would be able to translate for me. Since he was a student, I knew he could probably do with a bit of spare cash.

Alfredo responded enthusiastically; he told me his Catholic aunt had recently hired a *bruja* from the Cusco suburb of Huasao to perform a ceremony before the opening of Incas Dreams. Apparently the ceremony had involved the use of various plants and herbs, water from seven rivers, and a human embryo acquired from the local hospital. I choked on my coffee.

Three hours later, in the back of a beaten-up old cab heading for Huasao, I told Alfredo why I'd come to Peru. I'd thought, by doing so, that I'd just be satisfying his curiosity, which bordered on nosiness. Instead, his eyes filled with tears. He took out his wallet and showed me a picture of his pretty young mother who, he told me, had died seven years earlier. The young man's pain flooded my heart.

Torrential rain beat down on the windscreen as we sat together, bonding silently in empathy and sorrow, as the taxi wound its way through the grubby, deluged Cusco suburbs. We turned into Huasao. The driver asked us where we wanted to be dropped off. Alfredo, who had been unable to get hold of his aunt, explained that our intention was to visit a *bruja* or *chamán*, but that we had no idea which one or where.

The driver suddenly pulled over and started chatting to a woman, who, it transpired, was his sister-in-law. He asked her to recommend the best *bruja* in town. She directed us to a dilapidated house across the road from a church, and said that the woman who lived there had an excellent reputation.

We knocked on the door. A couple of snot-nosed Quechua kids in filthy clothes peeped around it and told us their mother was out. We'd just begun to walk away when we saw a very plump, scruffy woman in her late thirties, with a screaming toddler hanging over her shoulder, puffing up the middle of the road towards us, her long black plaits swinging from side to side. As she got closer I noticed stains on her grey smock.

Her appearance startled me. Over the years I'd seen numerous documentaries depicting semi-naked South American shamans in the Amazon jungle with needles through their cheeks and painted chests but I hadn't, as yet, seen any urban ones. Nor had I seen any *brujas* – not even in the Witches' Park in Cachiche. In my mind's eye I'd anticipated interviewing a slightly more exotic, mysterious-looking witch – not one with a broomstick and a pointy hat exactly, but perhaps a feather headdress, leopard-skin skirt or at the very least, a crystal necklace or two. However, it was too late to say anything to Alfredo, who was already explaining to the woman that I wanted a consultation.

She offloaded the baby onto the other kids and led us down some steps into a dark, smelly, windowless basement room with a concrete floor, illuminated by a dingy light bulb. On the wall hung a picture of the Indian guru, Sai

Baba, and a photograph of the Pope; perched on a narrow ledge beneath them both was a small statue of the Buddha. An official-looking framed certificate hung by the door. Alfredo examined it and declared that she was indeed the genuine article.

We sat on either side of a rickety cloth-covered table on which lay a couple of hundred coca leaves and a bell. I was instructed to pick up the leaves and scatter them. I felt both sceptical and anxious as the witch proceeded to silently study the pattern they'd settled into. She started to speak very quickly, in an unfamiliar dialect. I was only able to glean about half of what she was saying, so I asked Alfredo to translate.

With her eyes fixed on the coca leaves, she told me I had two jobs. Correct: I was (and still am) a psychotherapist and a writer. My husband and I were very different. True. I was a strong woman and my work and health were good, but sometimes I felt fearful, and had problems in the stomach. I laughed and said yes, I'd certainly had plenty of those since being in Peru.

I took out Sacha's photograph and passed it to her. She studied it carefully for a few moments, then looked me sorrowfully in the eyes. She said that my son was a very good person, and very handsome, but that someone – a man – did him a great harm. She pointed to her head, and said that this man had given him bad psychological problems. She also said that his separation from a woman he cared deeply for had caused my son pain in his heart. That would be Rebecca.

I started to cry, and explained Sacha's connection with Machu Picchu and how I was on my way there to scatter his ashes. She told me she herself was descended from the Incas, and that Machu Picchu was definitely the right place to be taking my son; his spirit would be returned to the *Apu* of Machu Picchu, the god who resides at the sacred tip of the mountain. She advised me to pray when scattering his ashes. I felt a powerful connection with her, with Alfredo, with Sacha. And I sensed, somehow, that she was delivering a message I was meant to hear – one that would strengthen my resolve to see this task through.

The Inca witch went on to suggest that I should write a book about Sacha and my travels in Peru. I told her I'd thought about it, and had been keeping a journal on the trip. She offered to perform a ritual for the success of the book and for my happiness. I agreed.

She left the room and returned ten minutes later with a collection of three dozen objects and laid them carefully on the table; a mixture of sweets, herbs, bits of coloured paper, wafers and a shrivelled, light brown embryo about two inches long – not of a human, she reassured me (thank God), but of an alpaca. She held up a little wax figure, saying it was me, and an orange wax car that she said was my car, and a little wax house that was my house.

After laying out the objects on the table, she recited incantations over them, rang the bell, and then wrapped them all up in cotton wool, whispering my name and David's into the bundle – for our happiness, she explained. She proceeded to wrap the bundle in expensive-looking paper, and then tied it together with a cotton strip.

Borrowing a pen from me, she drew an arrow to indicate the point at which the smoke would need to come out of the package to mingle with the spirits when it was burnt, then touched me all over with the package and made me breathe into it three times. She placed it carefully in a plastic bag and explained that later she would burn it on a grill.

I would have good health, she announced, and my work would go well, but people would be envious of me. Given that I was reeling from profound loss at the time, I found her last pronouncement pretty incomprehensible. Handing me a couple of dried beans, she said I should keep them in my purse for financial good fortune.

I asked if I could interview her and she agreed. I learnt that her name was Dionisia Quispe, and that she was thirty-nine years old and had three children. Dionisia told me she'd lived in Huasao all her life, and had begun practising her craft when she was very young. Her husband of fifteen years was a shaman, and he'd also taught her a great deal. The two hundred coca leaves, she explained, were like a book: she 'read' the patterns they fell into.

I had a strong sense she was illiterate, but didn't like to ask. I did ask, however, what the bell was for. She explained that its chimes summoned the spirits; they smelled the bag burning on the grill and then went about their business. Dionisia told me she enjoyed her job, and that we were lucky it was a Tuesday, as Tuesdays and Fridays were the days she held consultations. I asked her why she only held them on those days. Her power was at its strongest on Tuesdays and

Fridays she replied, because then, her spirit was clean and energised.

I inwardly chastised myself for, yet again, being too quick to make a shallow judgement based on appearance alone. Dionisia's scruffy clothes, ramshackle house and filthy kids belied her very genuine power, kindness and insight. I liked her, and felt gratified to have made a connection with someone of Inca descent whose ancestors' sacred citadel was soon to become my son's final resting place.

Outside in the blinding daylight, Alfredo and I took pictures of each other on the steps of the church opposite Dionisia's house. In the taxi on our way back into town, we both admitted to feeling quite dazed by the intensity of the experience. Like me, Alfredo had found it unnerving, fascinating and moving. I thanked him for his help. I'd taken an initial dislike to this young man, but now I felt deep warmth towards him. When the taxi dropped him off at his college, Alfredo and I enjoyed a long maternal/filial hug.

Still in a Dionisia daze, I arrived back at Incas Dreams where the receptionist was waiting to give me an urgent message from Roberto: I was to meet him immediately at a nearby restaurant. Although I'd felt ambivalent about seeing him again, on receiving this summons, I was relieved he'd made it.

I naturally assumed he'd checked into the room I'd reserved for him at Incas Dreams, and I was surprised to be told by the receptionist that he was staying at a hotel five minutes' walk away called *Sueños des Incas* – Incas Dreams in Spanish. A few moments of confusion followed until the penny dropped. I had been speaking Spanish when I rang his sister in Bogotá – unaware of the existence of a Cusco hotel with the same name as my hostel but in the other language. The receptionist at *Sueños des Incas* had apparently been calling around Cusco all morning, on Roberto's behalf, trying to locate me. I laughed as I cancelled his booking.

The receptionist warned me that the restaurant I was heading for was one of the priciest in Cusco. When I walked through the door, the contrast between Dionisia Quispe's dark, smelly coca-leafed basement and this light, tastefully modern upmarket eatery was delightfully disorientating.

Roberto seemed pleased to see me and we greeted each other with unaccustomed warmth. True to form, he ordered a bottle of the most expensive French wine on the list.

Since our divorce after three short years of marriage, we'd only ever seen each other in England, France or Africa. Now, for the first time in many years, we were together in South America again, and it felt strangely normal. He'd lost weight since I'd last seen him in the spring. His dark hair was greyer at the temples, but over the years he'd managed to retain his Latin American good looks – although quite how, given his unsaintly lifestyle, remained a mystery.

This was Roberto's first time in Peru and his excitement was infectious. He told me he remembered, as a child, his father returning once from Cusco with a bagful of silver jewellery for his mother. Roberto was fluent in English and it felt good, as I gave him a blow-by-blow account of my trip so far, to be nattering away in my natural lingo, dipping into my preferred colloquialisms and blasphemies for the first time in weeks. He nodded intently as he picked away at his *lomo saltado* – marinated stir-fried sirloin – and I devoured the best meal I'd had so far in Peru: *paiche*, the largest freshwater fish in the world from the Amazon River, and coconut rice.

Roberto pushed away his half-eaten plate of food and lit another cigarette. Following a stroke and a heart attack, he'd switched, reluctantly, to menthol. He'd always been a smoker.

I'd just turned nineteen when Robert and I first met, on a coach travelling from Bristol to London. There were two empty seats, one next to a greasy-haired, middle-aged woman in a brown raincoat who was reading the Bible, and the other beside a handsome, bearded, black-haired foreigner in jeans, chain-smoking Marlboros and reading the *Sunday Times*. There was no contest.

I'd been visiting my boyfriend Pete – soon to become my ex – in Bristol. A former politics student at Birmingham University, Pete had just returned from Madrid, where he'd been learning Spanish with a view to going out to Bolivia to fight with the left-wing guerrillas who continued to fight on after the execution of Che Guevara by the Bolivian military. Ever since I'd met him three years earlier Pete had been trying his hardest to make a right-on leftie out of me, which had subliminally manifested in my having a mad crush on the late Che Guevara.

In Roberto, who was fourteen years older than me, I believed I'd hit the jackpot: my very own Che. OK, so he was from Colombia instead of Argentina, and an architect rather than a doctor, but he was still a handsome South American who spoke convincingly about his concern for the plight of *los pobres*.

Only later did I learn that when he'd applied for a job in Cuba, the Cuban ambassador in London had wined, dined and Cuban-cigared him for weeks on end, before telling him he was far too middle-class to live and work out there. Apart from enjoying all the good things in life, as the ambassador himself clearly did, Roberto had made the mistake of recalling, after they'd had a few drinks one night, the wild, decadent times he and his brothers had enjoyed when they'd flown from their hometown of Barranquilla to Havana, for pre-revolution Batista-era fun weekends.

Roberto's mother Elvira cried tears of relief when he rang to tell her he'd finally found the woman he wanted to marry. She told him that she just *knew* I was '*rubia*' (blonde). Well, she was in for a big disappointment. Despite my protestations, Roberto sent her a plane ticket to London around the time of Sacha's birth, and she stayed with us for three long months. Although she drank tea every day of her life, Elvira had never made a pot of it herself; that was the maid's job. She was so proud of the mousy-blonde hair of her two nieces, who deigned to stay with us while they were touring Europe. They did little except criticise my nascent mothering skills.

In hindsight, poor Elvira must have been really unhappy at that time. Roberto's father was a well-respected colonel in the Colombian army. Resembling a tall, thin General Pinochet, his politics veered more to the left. In his earlier life, he'd hung out in cafés and bars with a circle of like-minded thinkers and writers, including the novelist, Gabriel García Márquez.

In a scenario worthy of a García Márquez plot, the colonel had only recently returned – with his tail between his legs – to the marital home, after running off to live on the family farm with a 24-year-old floozy. To make matters worse, Roberto's sister, who had three small children, had also been abandoned by her husband. Following his father-in-law's example, the latter had decided to shack up with the sister of the colonel's girlfriend. Unlike his father-in-law's, his desertion was permanent.

When Roberto took me and baby Sacha on holiday to Colombia, I came to understand that Elvira and her Basque-descended family put light-haired, light-skinned people on a pedestal as 'pure-blooded class'. Sacha was a very pale-skinned baby, and Elvira would proudly show off her grandson's whiteness to all and sundry; perhaps it compensated for her daughter-in-law not being blonde. She worshipped baby Sacha, and would spend hours gently rocking him from side to side, whispering into his ear, '*Corazón de melón, melón. Corazón de melón, melón.*' ('Heart of melon, melon.')

As for the disgraced colonel, he vehemently disapproved of us naming our son Sacha – '*nombre de mujer!*' ('a woman's name!') – instead of Roberto. Sacha was the first son of the first son, and so was expected to carry the male Christian name.

Years later, Sacha arrived in Barranquilla one summer to discover news crews camped outside the family home and, inside, his *abuelo* on his deathbed. Sacha hurried to the bedside; the old colonel greeted him warmly, and then, yet again, made a point of expressing his disapproval of his grandson's Christian name.

As Roberto chewed on his *maracuya* (passion fruit) and ice-cream dessert, reluctantly eyeing his fags, I registered how this broken link in the family line must have compounded his pain at losing Sacha.

Roberto ordered another bottle of wine and – ever Mr Macho – launched into his well-worn and embarrassing flirt routine with the young waitress. I couldn't help but remember the weekend when, during that trip to Colombia, we'd left Sacha with his grandparents and gone to stay with Alvaro, a friend of Roberto's.

On a visit to London, Alvaro had fallen in love with my sister Suzanne. When we arrived on his doorstep, he burst into tears because I reminded him of Suzanne. He confessed that, for months, he'd nurtured the hope that we would bring her with us as a surprise. For the whole nightmare weekend, Alvaro never stopped crying, as I was a constant reminder of his lost love. At breakfast the next morning, he decided to drown his sorrows by getting disgustingly drunk on *aguardiente*, and Roberto generously agreed to keep him company. In this alcohol-fuelled condition, Alvaro insisted on driving us over terrifyingly high mountain passes and dirt roads to the *hacienda* of a friend whose wife had recently left him for another man. It wasn't difficult to understand why; the 'friend' was a vicious alcoholic with a psychopathic personality.

The autumn before, in a childish fit of pique over Roberto taking his mother to Paris for a week instead of me, I went to Amsterdam with Sacha and had a short fling with a Dutch friend of Roberto's. Although I'd apparently been 'forgiven' my treachery, the *aguardiente* and female-fuelled misery of Alvaro and his cuckolded friend stirred it all up again. In true 1970s Colombian style, the three men lolled around on the *hacienda* hammocks, bonding in their misogyny and becoming increasingly drunk. I didn't want to join them, nor did I want to sit with our host's miserable, monosyllabic mother and her canasta-playing, embroidering female entourage. Noticing I was bored, our host kept taunting me, calling me '*la reina*' ('the queen'). He suggested I ride one of the *hacienda* horses: a particular stallion he assured me was safe. I was settling myself in the saddle when, to his great amusement, it bolted and I was thrown off. I was badly bruised but I could have broken my neck.

That night, our host invited us out for a drink. He took us to a massive saloon in the middle of the countryside. I felt his choice of bar was as deliberate as his choice of horse.

A hundred or so inebriated *hombres* were there and I was the only *mujer*. Outside in the yard, a couple of blood-curdling cockfights were in progress. I found the drunken macho vibe even more frightening when Roberto joined in with the mocking chant of the psychopath's ever-increasing entourage, many of whom were his employees: *'la reina, la reina.'* In retrospect, I don't think he had much choice but, somewhere along the line, I felt he wasn't protecting me and it put another knife into our increasingly fragile relationship.

The age difference had also started to bite. Back in Barranquilla, I struck up a friendship with Roberto's aunt Hilda, a highly educated, sensitive woman who worked as a librarian to support her family after the sudden death of her debt-ridden husband.

Hilda worshipped the ground on which her son, Henrique, walked. Green-eyed, charming and closer to my age than Roberto, Henrique had an illegitimate son a few months older than Sacha. The chemistry between Henrique and me was inconveniently mutual and we spent a few glorious days together on a deserted Caribbean beach, but that was as far as it went. I was at University College, London and he dreamed of studying for a master's degree at the London School of Economics. When we returned home, I sent him the prospectus, but Hilda couldn't afford the fees.

This was to prove tragic, and Hilda and I were destined to have more in common than we could ever have possibly imagined. A couple of years after my return from Colombia,

207

her beloved Henrique was killed by the Colombian mafia for flirting with the girlfriend of a drug baron. His body was dumped on the local rubbish tip.

Roberto and I didn't discuss this sad memory as we sipped our brandies, nor did we talk much about Sacha or the painful task ahead of us. For once, I managed to ignore *los pobres* outside. But it wasn't only the food and the alcohol, or the relief of meeting up with Roberto that had lifted my spirits; it was also my illuminating and moving encounter with Dionisia Quispe, the Inca witch.

# gringo bill's

## another mother

The PeruRail backpacker train pulled out of Cusco station at 6.30am for the four-hour journey to Agua Caliente; three-quarters of an hour later, it was still slowly zigzagging its way up and around Cusco's cosy back streets and lush, interminable terraces. I was impatient to leave Cusco behind, to continue my journey.

In the crowded train carriage everyone was asleep except me. Although I'd been up since 4.30am, I was determined to stay awake and take in the stunning scenery. Slumped beside me, an unshaven Roberto, smelling of fags and booze, was snoring quietly. I revelled in the solitude. Both quantum cosmology and Buddhism tell us that we're all interconnected. At times for me this concept is positively awesome; at others, positively awful.

The night porter had forgotten my early morning wake-up call. Thankfully, I'd woken up in time anyway. But Roberto was so late arriving to collect me in the taxi we'd pre-booked from his hotel that we leaped onto the train with only seconds to spare. Rather shamefaced, he confessed he'd been out clubbing the night before, and had only slept for two hours. Not bad going for a sixty-four-year-old with a heart condition. How did he manage it, I wondered, not without a tad of admiration.

Over the last two days in Cusco, we'd tiptoed cautiously around each other's constantly shifting moods. '*Roberto es muy nervioso,*' his mother always used to say. Well, I was starting to feel nervous about Roberto's alcohol consumption and irascible mindset. He'd been impossibly impatient at times – storming out of banks because he refused to wait in a queue. Since working in Lagos, like many ex-pats out there, he'd become a heavy drinker. Losing Sacha clearly hadn't helped.

Our meals together were emotional and intense, as we found ourselves going over and over our son's life and death. I needed to fill him in on painful details, such as the inquest, and what, at that time, appeared to be the abortive search for the paedophile. Roberto, like me, was still in the depths of grief, eased only by sometimes feeling Sacha's spirit around him, and by alcohol.

But we'd still managed some civilised Cusco sightseeing and shopping together. Roberto had insisted on buying a beautiful alpaca bedspread and two colourful hand-woven rugs from a couple of pre-pubescent girls in a market who had haggled away like a pair of old women. Then he'd given them to me.

Our last day in Cusco was frenetic, what with sorting out hotels, Roberto's return flight and searching for a bank with a short queue. Stress sprang up from unexpected quarters. After settling my bill at Incas Dreams in the morning, I'd asked the pretty girl on reception if she could arrange for us to be met at the station in Machu Picchu town by someone from the hostel where we'd be staying. She said, smiling warmly, that she'd describe me as *'una chica alta y linda'* (a tall, lovely girl).

Such flattery came at a price, especially at Christmas. That evening she knocked on the door of my room while I was sorting out final travel arrangements with Roberto. He'd had the obligatory flirt with her when we collected my key, and she could see he'd had a few to drink. Fluttering her eyelashes at him, she said her books were out because I'd underpaid her that morning by 50 sol.

I remembered checking the bill very carefully with her and settling it, equally carefully, in cash. She had a guilty air about her. She knew I knew she was lying. Roberto took out his wallet. I remonstrated. It was my room after all, and my responsibility. Close to 'tears', she said she hadn't been paid yet and couldn't make the money up. Not wanting Roberto to pay and not in the mood for conflict, I shoved the 50 sol she was demanding into her hand and shunted her out.

I was also starting to feel strangely inundated by husbands – previous and current. Rebecca had wanted me to email her about the scattering arrangements. In the internet café I'd noticed that ex-husband Jake and current husband David had sent me long emails that I wasn't able to reply to, as previous ex-husband Roberto had plonked himself beside me at the computer. When I finally got around to packing my suitcase, after midnight, I caught myself thinking that Sacha would have found all this hilarious.

As the train began to pick up speed, a Mexican father and his two teenage sons, dozing opposite us, began to stir. One of the lads took an Andean whistle from his pocket and started to blow into it. The shrill discordant notes so early in the morning, from a wind instrument he had no idea how to play, made my head throb. I hadn't been clubbing like Roberto, but I was, nevertheless, feeling a bit jaded after accompanying him on a couple of his bacchanalian outings.

As Cusco finally vanished from sight, it dawned on me that the stress I was feeling wasn't only due to the irritating behaviour of interconnected others, but also because, having focused solely on my own grief for the past weeks, over the last few days I'd become a conduit for the grief of others. And I was feeling responsible, albeit misplaced, for Roberto, and for the 'success' of the task ahead.

Unable to stand any more of the piercing Andean whistle, I glared at the kid opposite and blurted out, *'por favor*!!!' He looked embarrassed and stopped playing immediately. Suddenly I saw myself through his eyes, and, realising that I must come across as the sort of arsey adult I used to hate when I was his age, smiled at him remorsefully.

I woke Roberto up as we entered the Sacred Valley, thinking he wouldn't want to miss out on such mind-blowing scenery. Not one of my best ideas. He had an enormous coughing fit, waking up any remaining sleepers in the carriage, then went straight back to sleep again. Oh shit! Was he getting ill? That was all I needed.

The mountainous, jungle landscape began to have a tranquillising effect on me. If it all goes horribly wrong from here on in, I reassured myself, there is nothing I can do about it. The train was getting close to the Inca Trail that Sacha had hiked, and the terrain looked challenging, to say the least. I remembered him telling me how his trail guide had pulled coca leaves off bushes, and instructed him to chew on them when the going got tough.

'Coca leaves are nothing like as potent as cocaine, Mum,' Sacha explained. 'They suppress your appetite and help your body acclimatise to the low-oxygenated Andean air.'

I was starting to look forward to arriving in the small town at the foothills of Machu Picchu, known as Aguas Calientes.

'What a strange name for a town, Hot Waters!' I commented to Roberto, when he began, at last, to stir. Gringo Bill's was an odd name for a hostel, too. Who was Bill? Would I meet him?

I'd made the booking via a frustratingly slow email correspondence with someone called Margarita. I couldn't take the risk of not having a definite place to stay for this vital last leg of the trip. I'd looked at a hotel, a very expensive one, at the entrance to Machu Picchu itself, but Jake warned me they'd 'accidentally' lost his booking when he'd been in Peru a few years earlier, and he'd had to bribe them to find it again.

We were met at the station by a couple of porters from Gringo Bill's sporting an oversized luggage trolley. It was a five-minute walk up, down and along the little alleyways to the hostel. A stray, well-fed-looking mongrel dog followed us there from the station. Over the next few days, he continued to follow me around the little town.

A colourful, hilly hotchpotch of a place, Aguas Calientes had winding streets, natural thermal springs and some interesting-looking shops and restaurants. Most tourists go to Machu Picchu just for the day, returning to Cusco on the backpacker train in the evening, which means they never really get to see the tiny town. What struck me as strange was that there were no cars or roads to speak of, only coaches taking people the eight kilometres up to Machu Picchu itself.

Gringo Bill's was overpriced but atmospheric. I particularly liked the mosaic designs on the terraces, the steep steps and the murals on the walls. I'd booked a couple of the best rooms for Roberto and myself. With the undertaking that lay ahead, I was determined to be as comfortable as possible. My room, at the top of the building, had a balcony that looked out over the town and some formidable, cloud-drenched mountains, which towered over an expansive sea of green. Wonderful. Wonderful, but wet.

Margarita, a pleasant, attractive Peruvian woman in her forties, told us it had been raining solidly for a week. She appeared to be running the place on her own. I suspected she was, or had once been, married to the absent American owner, Gringo Bill. She recommended a restaurant that served typical Peruvian food. As the rain lashed down outside, we slurped one of its specialities, hot potato soup, relieved to have made it thus far. Machu Picchu no longer felt beyond reach.

By late afternoon, it was clear that Roberto had developed a bronchial infection, aggravated by the altitude and, no doubt, his late-night clubbing and smoking. He refused to see a doctor. I began to feel genuinely concerned that he wouldn't manage the Machu Picchu terraces. To scatter the ashes, we'd need to get away from the tourist areas, and that would involve a certain amount of climbing.

We agreed I'd go there on my own the following day and do a recce. Roberto returned to the hostel to lie down, and I headed for the ticket hall in the town, where I discovered it certainly wasn't cheap to visit Machu Picchu. I bought one ticket for 31st December and two for 2nd January.

I popped into a wildlife exhibition in the same building. Wandering around it, I began to understand why the Incas, who were pantheists and worshipped Pachamama (Mother Earth),had selected Machu Picchu as their main centre of worship.

This humid, biodiverse region of thundering rivers and crystalline waterfalls was home to 403 types of bird, 352 varieties of butterfly, forty-one species of mammals and thirteen species of river creatures. Its gene pools, ecosystems and impressive diversity of flora and fauna were among the largest not just in South America but also the world: a paradise for wildlife explorers and botanists. These Incas knew what they were doing.

On arriving back at Gringo Bill's, I could hear Roberto at the reception desk talking excitedly to Margarita. My heart sank when I realised he'd told her the reason why we'd come to Machu Picchu. I wasn't at all pleased. I didn't want the entire hostel knowing why we were there. I'd hoped to remain an anonymous tourist; I didn't want anybody's pity.

Approaching them warily, I was surprised to see that Margarita's face was wet with tears. She told me that her own son, William, had died five years earlier in a car crash at the age of seven, and that she still had his ashes on her mantelpiece. We commiserated on the pain of losing a child. I surmised that William was probably Gringo Bill's son. Perhaps his death explained Bill's absence, but I didn't want to ask. Many couples separate after the death of a child, because their mutual grief is too unbearable.

Little William, Margarita told us, was always thinking of others and was too kind for this world. Although adamant that she couldn't bear to part with his ashes, she was intrigued that we'd come halfway around the world to scatter Sacha's at the sacred citadel on her doorstep. The sacred citadel where, she said, little William loved to play every Sunday.

I sat on my balcony that evening staring down at the reflections of the street lights in the puddles on the plaza below, thinking about Alfredo and his mother, and Margarita and her son; this was the type of interconnectedness I found awesome. While my heart went out to Margarita, there was a strange comfort in knowing that I wasn't alone. Another mother had lost her son. Loss was ubiquitous.

Margarita smiled at me as I handed her my key and told her I was on my way up to Machu Picchu to do a recce. I was lucky, she said, because it was the first day for a week that the sun had shone.

At Machu Picchu, I leaped off the coach and made a beeline for the very top of the high southern terraces. I wanted to have an overview of Machu Picchu and Huayna Picchu – the famous aerial postcard view. I climbed so high that I was able to get completely away from the tourists. Apart from the odd grazing alpaca, the closest living human being was about twenty metres below me, smoking a spliff.

Once the ashes had made it into Peru without being tampered with at customs, my anxiety had focused on finding a place to scatter them that was away from the main tourist drag; now I also had to find somewhere that was accessible on level ground that Roberto could hack. I was determined that Sacha's ashes weren't going to be trampled on by walking boots or Nike trainers, and that Roberto wasn't going to have another stroke. What was the point of travelling this great distance for random desecration, or another death?

As my eyes darted about hunting for a suitable scattering spot, I sensed that Sacha was beside me. My mind stopped buzzing, and I began to marvel at the electrifying, sun-soaked beauty of the peaks and terraces of the Lost City of the Incas. It was New Year's Eve and I'd made it to Machu Picchu.

The previous New Year's Eve was the last time I'd seen Sacha alive. He'd looked really happy when he opened his front door. I hadn't particularly felt like going down to Brighton that day, but the girls in the upstairs flat were moving out.

Sacha had used the shaver/beard trimmer I'd given him for Christmas and now had a very light moustache and tightly trimmed goatee that made him look more like his old self. His eyes were shining and he was getting ready to party big-time for New Year. I lent him my phone as his was out of credit. As I pulled weeds out of the front garden while waiting for the girls to finish their packing, I could hear him making New Year calls, talking excitedly to long-lost friends about how he was 'getting sorted'.

Mikey had found a girl who could move into the downstairs flat in January and look after the dogs while Sacha was visiting his father in Africa. Sacha rang a friend with a van and asked if he could help, the following week, to clear out some of his junk to make space for this new arrival in the flat. Some other friends wanted Sacha to meet them in London to party. This would have meant leaving the dogs; there was a party happening in Brighton, too. Concerned about lonely, barking dogs and complaining neighbours, I asked him not to go to London, and he didn't. Would it have made any difference if he had done? Life is so full of 'what ifs' when you've lost someone.

Now, exactly a year later, I needed to find a suitable place to scatter his ashes. He understood that too, and 'showed' me where: the other side of the plateau, the point in the distance where Huayna Picchu peak intersected with the smaller peak of Machu Picchu. He 'told' me that, whenever I pictured his lifeless body, I should visualise this glorious vista instead. I looked down at the spell-binding city of granite built by Pachachutec (He who Shakes the Earth), the most revered Inca ruler. Then I looked across the verdant ravines, to the peaks of Salcantay and Cerro San Gabriel. Sacha had so loved climbing mountains.

Feeling at peace, I took some photographs and headed back down around the southern terraces and along the top edge of the Urubamba Valley. Aware that he was guiding me, I veered off towards the northern terraces and then on to the Sacred Rock: a lump of granite, the shape of which is said to resemble the mountain of Putukusi, another sacred Inca site towering to the east.

Not far behind the Sacred Rock were a bamboo gate and a wooden booth. Inside the booth sat the guardian – the Peruvian equivalent of a Health and Safety Officer. He instructed me to sign my name in a book, because people were sometimes injured ascending the peaks, or bitten by poisonous snakes. Once inside the gate, there were two paths. I 'knew' I had to take the path to the left.

After a fairly gentle climb, I came across some low boulders which I clambered over easily. I looked around. I was well away from the main tourist drag and there wasn't a person in sight. A little further on, I found a shady, tree-strewn alcove with a flat stone plateau that overlooked a steep drop down the forested slope of Huayna Picchu. The place was perfect. Roberto would find the climb manageable, and no tourist could possibly ascend or descend the sharp mountain drop where we could safely scatter the ashes. Sacha had chosen well.

An hour later, eating lunch outside a riverside café in Aguas Calientes with 'Hey Jude' blasting away at full volume, I felt euphoric. I'd had the good fortune to see Machu Picchu, easily the most spiritually electrifying place I'd visited on this planet, in glorious sunshine. And without any shadow of a doubt, I'd felt Sacha's guiding presence. So the dead, I reaffirmed to myself, do speak to the living.

Back at the hostel, in my excitement, I managed to pull the outside handle off my door. Margarita was sweet about it and said she'd get a guy to come and fix it straight away. I found Roberto in his room and launched into a rapturous description of my recce, thinking that my enthusiasm would excite him too. But he became very quiet, and began walking around in circles, smoking agitatedly. Then he stubbed out his cigarette, put on his jacket and hurried out.

The workman took nearly three hours to replace the handle. God only knew why. I had no choice but to remain in my room while he was fixing it. I sat on the balcony writing up my journal, worrying that Roberto was drinking. There was no need. He eventually appeared at my door, completely sober, and told me he'd felt so overwhelmed with emotion following my description of Machu Picchu that he'd needed to be alone, and had sat outside a café in the main square for hours, drinking coffee. Reminding me that it was New Year's Eve, he told me he'd booked a table in a restaurant and ordered champagne.

We hit Aguas Calientes. My mood was still good. The demi-sec champagne turned out to be Peruvian and tasted like cheap *Asti Spumante*, but we still enjoyed it. The restaurant was vibrant and the music upbeat. We talked politics, life, religion and the origins of the universe until the discussion returned, inevitably, to Sacha.

Roberto told me the happiest times he'd ever spent were with his son. He recalled his guilt over an abortive trip Sacha had made to Colombia, some years earlier. The two of them were supposed to meet up, but Roberto kept delaying his arrival due to work. When he finally did appear, it was already time for Sacha to leave. They'd had a big argument in a hotel in Bogotá. Roberto said Sacha had broken down in tears, saying that the only reason he'd come to Colombia was to see his father.

Roberto went on to confess to feeling bad that, although he'd given Sacha money, he'd basically washed his hands of his drug and mental health issues, leaving me to deal with it all. I was both surprised and relieved to hear this. I'd always wanted some sort of an acknowledgement of his lack of involvement with Sacha's problems, which had fuelled my anger towards him over the years, and he clearly needed to get this off his chest. Roberto wasn't the kind of guy who said 'sorry' very often.

What was also painfully clear was how deeply he loved his son, and how bereft and lonely he felt without him. I acknowledged the pain I must have caused Roberto when I left him and how, if I'd been less selfish and had tried harder to make the relationship work, Sacha might have had a more stable childhood.

As we sat there, staring down at the main square and its majestic statue of Pachacutec, I felt so sad for Roberto that my deep-seated resentment towards him finally dissipated. I decided to forgive myself, too. And to forgive Sacha for not trying harder to stay clean.

As midnight approached, we left the restaurant and went down to the square. The excitement of the New Year was everywhere. Inside the church, Mass was being held. Entire families with babies, young children and grandparents prayed together as fireworks exploded outside. Roberto and I didn't have much to celebrate – only this new-found honesty and empathy between us. We moved onto a bar, ordering wine and some pancakes. At midnight, the staff threw confetti all over us. We laughed at the irony of it.

The rain came cascading down as we made our way back to Gringo Bill's a couple of hours later. We arrived, drenched to the skin, only to find the door locked. We rang and rang and knocked and knocked, finally waking up a scowling Swede, who let us in. Thinking all the guests were tucked up in bed, the night porter had deserted his post to join in the fun somewhere. The Swede made sure he was in trouble with Margarita the next day.

# in hot water

### holocaust memorial day

On the afternoon of New Year's Day, we wandered up to the natural thermal spring baths at the top of Aguas Calientes. It was a lovely, gentle, riverside climb in the shade of green mountains covered in cloud forest. The mineral-rich springs had been channelled into a couple of small, communal, outdoor baths. Fortunately, there were only a few people sharing the baths and they were mainly locals. I tried, unsuccessfully, to persuade Roberto to join me for a therapeutic soak but, exhausted by the climb and still coughing his lungs up, he parked himself on the veranda and ordered a beer.

As my body floated around in the comforting, womb-like thermal bath, I was aware that my mind, too, was suspended in a kind of limbo: poised between the anniversary of my last seeing Sacha alive, and the anniversary of his death to come. The waters were calm and soporific but 'being in hot water' could also mean finding yourself in a difficult place which spelled trouble. I was afraid that, much like this time the year before, I might soon be immersed in the uncharted waters of the unpredictable emotions that accompany grief.

Sacha stayed in Brighton on New Year's Eve, as I'd asked him to, rather than leave the dogs and go partying in London. From what I could piece together later, he went to an all-night party/rave in a field outside the city, where he mainly hung out with a friend called Jimmy who lived in Brighton with his pregnant girlfriend, Julie. That evening, Jimmy had asked Sacha to be godfather to their baby, which must have thrilled him.

It took Jimmy a few days – urged on by Sacha's friend Emma – to pluck up the courage to call me with details of their final hours together. When he finally did so, he told me they'd taken cocaine at the party and had been drinking a great deal, staying up all night and having 'a blinding time'. Sacha had left Jimmy on New Year's Day, saying he was going to pop in on Mikey, who was still on crutches, to see if he needed anything and then go home to sort out the dogs. Mikey was out. Jimmy and Sacha had agreed to meet up in a pub that evening. But Sacha never appeared.

Even though I hadn't managed to get through to Sacha on his mobile for a day or two, I wasn't concerned. Sacha not answering his phone was nothing unusual; the fact that he was always running out of credit or losing it had become something of a joke. Sally had even bought him boxer shorts with pictures of mobile phones on them. He'd been really happy over Christmas and on New Year's Eve when I'd last seen him, and was so looking forward to going to Africa.

As I drove over to Brighton to help Sacha make space for the girl who would be moving in to look after the dogs, my mind, like many other people's, was full of the spectre of the devastating, watery deaths caused by the tsunami in South East Asia. There was no reply when I rang on the doorbell, so I let myself in and called out Sacha's name. The dogs were barking. The television was on. I called his name again. The door to the living room swung open. The dogs came rushing out.

I saw Sacha slumped over on the floor in kneeling position, still dressed in the same black T-shirt and green trousers he'd been wearing on New Year's Eve. There was no sense of his presence in that room, or in the house, which in a detached way felt strange. His body was an empty shell. Sacha's spirit had already left; of that I was certain. I also knew instinctively that he'd decided to have one last party blow-out, before finally getting clean.

The dogs leapt all over me. In a trance, I let them out into the garden and called David. He was in the car on his way back from working overnight at the BBC. I was so calm, so calm, so very, very calm. I even warned him of speed traps I'd noticed on the A23. I'd rehearsed Sacha's death so many times in my head. David couldn't take it in. I had to repeat the words: 'Sacha's dead. Sacha's dead. Dead. Yes, he's dead. Dead.'

I went back inside and called the police. After a quarter of an hour, they still hadn't arrived. I called again and screamed down the phone at them to come immediately.

Ten minutes later, a couple of young coppers turned up on the doorstep and just stood there asking me the same questions over and over again.

'What's his name?'

'What's your relationship?'

'When did you last see him alive?'

Couldn't they see I was in shock? I walked upstairs to the empty flat and called my parents. My mother answered the phone. When I told her the news she screamed, 'No!'

David arrived and burst into floods of tears. But I couldn't cry. We sat in the living room of the flat upstairs, staring down at the hideous blue carpet, holding hands in stunned silence. I was living through my worst nightmare, and there was a horrible familiarity to it all. Downstairs, Sacha's flat was milling with police. A plain-clothes policeman, who said he worked for the coroner, came upstairs and pulled off a pair of sinister-looking rubber gloves. My heart was pounding. He gave me his card, telling me I could call him at any time.

David told me not to look out of the living room window, because they were carrying Sacha's body into the mortuary van.

Despite their personal grief, my loving parents insisted on moving in to take care of me. They'd each lost a young brother and remembered only too well the anguish their mothers had suffered after one had died from heart failure at the age of eighteen and the other, a young pilot, had been shot down during the Battle of Britain.

'Look, flowers, darling.'

'Look, more beautiful flowers have arrived. People are so kind.'

'Look at this lovely bouquet of flowers.'

My poor mother was trying her best to cheer me up. Each time I entered my living room, which smelt like a hybrid brothel/funeral parlour, more flowers had appeared. Bouquets in makeshift vases had even infiltrated the kitchen. In the week following Sacha's death, the doorbell rang persistently with yet another delivery. I would sniff each bouquet politely and read the card, secretly thinking to myself: I don't want fucking pink carnations or fucking white lilies or fucking yellow roses or fucking blue orchids. I want my son back.

What held a little more meaning were the eucalyptus tree and the rowan tree, given by friends, which swayed in large pots on the patio, waiting to be planted. Sacha wasn't a cut-flowery person and neither was I. We liked our flowers in the wild.

I spent much of my time staring out of the French windows into the garden, watching birds and clouds drift across the sky. The lyrics to 'I'm Free' from The Who's album *Tommy* kept going through my head, along with the musical refrain, 'On the road again... der der der der der der...' I had no idea where that one came from or who it was by.

David and I discussed music for the funeral. He claimed Sacha had liked the band Canned Heat and that he'd often had to put the CD away after Sacha had stayed with us. David thought he must have listened to it for the harmonica parts. David played the CD: *On the road again... der der der der der der* came blaring out. In the song, recorded in 1968, the singer tells his mamma that he's so sick of cryin' he's going out on the road again, and asks her to cry no more.

I was later to learn that the lead singer and harmonica player, Alan Wilson, had died of a heroin overdose...der der der der der der...

The relentless misery I was feeling was only alleviated by the occasional brief moment of relief that Sacha wouldn't have to suffer any more from voices and cravings. I knew the overdose was unintentional. One last partying fling before he got clean.

But would it have been? Heroin had got its claws into him and, in times of catastrophe, it would have been his first calling card. Full recovery from schizophrenia was rare, and it was very possible that I could have become a permanent carer. But even that would have been infinitely preferable to the pain of this grief. I simply wanted him back.

Following the autopsy, Sacha's body was released and taken to the funeral parlour at the end of our road. The white, open coffin was on display in the tiny chapel. Because his body had to remain in a sealed bag, we asked the undertaker to lay some clothes over him – his best black trousers and a Headflux T-shirt, made by his own company, of which he'd been so proud. In the coffin, we placed his harmonica, the crystal that Rebecca had kept in her bra for several days beforehand, and large photographs of Sacha's beloved dogs, Dodge and Ruff.

Phil presented me with a gorgeous watercolour of a lotus. The night he learned of Sacha's death, in the depths of his own grief, he stayed up all night painting it for me. I understood why he'd been Sacha's best friend. While I've come to truly appreciate the generosity and kindness behind everyone's Interflora gestures, Phil's lotus was the only flower that truly touched my heart.

I waved at Roberto, who was downing his second beer, and smiled at a pair of filthy, exhausted, happy-looking backpacker girls who were washing their hair under the taps. They must have just completed the Inca Trail. I wondered whether Sacha, too, had bathed in these thermal springs.

I didn't want to leave my lovely, peaceful limbo bath. The day and night before had been so surprisingly good, I'd almost gone into denial about the real purpose of my trip. What was the next day going to bring? What would I be thinking and feeling as I scattered my son's ashes? And once they'd been scattered, would it be a release, or would the loss of all that was physically left of him shatter me?

I hated not knowing, feeling unprepared; a stream of anxiety flowed silently in. Einstein claimed that only a genius can live with uncertainty. I'd created the framework within which all this could happen, but what if it went horribly wrong? What if a party of noisy tourists barged in on our private ceremony? What if an official spied on us? There were laws against scattering ashes in some countries, especially at historical sites. I'd never scattered ashes before. Apart from my grandparents, nobody really close to me had ever died. I had no road map for this journey.

Enough! I dragged myself out of the thermal bath, laid my towel on a patch of grass in the sun, set my iPod on random play and closed my eyes. The Polish composer Henryk Górecki's poignant third symphony, an evocation of the Holocaust, came on. I certainly wasn't in the mood to go there, so I quickly switched to some chill-out music instead. But the seed had already been sown. By ironic co-incidence, 27th January, Holocaust Memorial Day, was also the day of Sacha's cremation. Yet again, I resisted this memory; struggled to block it out. But, like a malignant magnet, it sucked me back in…

I'm in the spare bedroom, watching my sister Sally change into a smart new flowery dress. Will she be warm enough in the crematorium? I decide not to ask. She's putting on such a brave face. I've asked her to read my tribute to Sacha during the service, because I'm afraid I'll crack up.

I'm wearing a cream trouser suit and a pink silk blouse. Black feels inappropriate. The hairdresser insisted on straightening my hair yesterday. The first time I ever had it straightened Sacha told me I looked like a character out of

*East Enders*. Everyone is commenting on how lovely I look; do they hope it will cheer me up? For some reason, I keep referring to the funeral as the wedding; an unconscious slip, I suppose. My marriage to David was the last time many of the people I've invited today came together.

The doorbell rings and I go downstairs. Roberto has arrived with Sacha's cousin Olga and her husband, who have flown in from Spain. Olga has just visited Sacha's coffin in the chapel of rest and can't stop crying. She tells me her mother is holding a Mass for Sacha in a church in Bogotá.

A courier appears, just in time. He hands me a bundle of leaflets from the street children's orphanage in Barranquilla, Roberto's birthplace. Sacha wouldn't want flowers. I'm going to take the leaflets to the funeral for people who wish to donate to the orphanage instead.

The mini-bus has pulled up outside. We all pile in. Suzanne holds my hand as we drive away. Sally comforts Roberto. I gaze numbly out of the window at the grey, leafless winter landscape.

We approach the crematorium. In the distance, I see a stationary black Mercedes. I don't connect that this is the hearse. There are trucks and vehicles in the car park, and young people of Sacha's age mill around the gardens. Many of them, I guess, are New Age Travellers. Rebecca tells me their friends have driven here from all over Europe. I notice two young men in dark suits standing awkwardly outside the entrance. Who are they? Then Suzanne waves and I recognise my nephews: Sacha's gentle cousins from Ireland have metamorphosed into his coffin bearers.

Inside the crematorium, Buddhist friends are busy preparing the altar and arranging the evergreen foliage, which for Buddhists represents the eternity of life. The leader of my Buddhist organisation walks over and hugs me. I've asked him to give the address, and he's assured me he'll give Sacha a good send-off. Tears start to well up, but I order them to stop. I don't want my make-up to run; I have to look my best for Sacha. I didn't stay up drinking wine with the others last night. I couldn't risk feeling under par today. I must be 100 per cent present. I'm determined I'm going to hold it together, because once I start crying these days, I can't stop.

Santana is playing.

Old friends and relatives are pouring into the chapel, some I recognise, but many of Sacha's friends I've never seen before. Suddenly it's standing room only.

I look anxiously around for Roberto. We dropped him off at the nearby pub, where he's arranged to meet his Colombian business partner, who is flying in from Paris. There he is, lurching up the aisle, staring at the floor. I motion for him to sit beside me. He doesn't look good. I'm in the front row, between Roberto and David – my past and my present. How strange. The main crematorium doors creak open. I swing around. Hundreds of pairs of eyes fix on me. I'm trapped in a fragment of some grotesque dream.

I watch as the eyes shift from me and alight on six young men, Sacha's friends and cousins, who are carrying a white cardboard coffin up the aisle. I'm peeved that the undertakers have put a blue cloth over the coffin. I've asked them to keep it bare, apart from the bouquet of flowers my mother has insisted on buying. Sacha would have wanted a plain white cardboard coffin. How dare they? I've organised it all so meticulously. I'm the director of this show.

The performance begins. But now I'm annoyed that our oh-so-carefully selected music isn't loud enough. I try to catch the eye of the elderly woman who is working the sound system, but she refuses to look up. The leader is giving the address. Random sound bites hit my ears.

*Death is but a state of latency, an interval like a night's sleep… Life is eternal and indestructible forever existing… Sacha understood, through his suffering, the laws of cause and effect and karma… Sacha is now in a state of Buddhahood…*

Brother Neil is clutching the tribute my nephew Alex has written. I've asked him to read it. He's chanting, but he isn't a Buddhist. How weird. I look around; other non-Buddhists appear to be spontaneously chanting, too.

*Nam Myoho Renge Kyo. Nam Myoho Renge Kyo. Nam Myoho Renge Kyo. Nam Myoho Renge Kyo. Nam Myoho Renge Kyo…*

Sally takes centre stage. She's smiling at the audience. I try to fix my gaze on her, and not on the white coffin to her right.

*Sacha was such a handsome devil, with the most beautiful*

*almond eyes… He appeared, even from a young age, full of so much wisdom…*

Sally pauses to look at me. She's going to read my tribute now. David squeezes my hand. Was I right to chicken out? Yes.

*Sacha was no angel… He could be a right stubborn little bugger sometimes… Sacha was a free spirit, with a generous heart and a great capacity to love… He was happiest when travelling in Europe and South America…*

The crematorium door slams shut. I jump up and look around. Someone whispers in my ear that an old school friend of Sacha's has run outside, in floods of tears.

*He loved climbing mountains and fishing… Sacha was a brilliant harmonica player…*

*On the road again… der der der der der der…*

Turn the music up, woman!

Rebecca's about to speak. She looks nervous, bless her.

*From the day we met we remained inseparable for seven years… He was an explorer… Within the physical as well as the spiritual realms of existence… Sacha would want us all to celebrate his life… He's here with us, all around us, laughing that cheeky laugh…*

Phil takes the stage. He's wearing a Headflux T-shirt; the same design as the one Sacha's wearing. No. Don't think about Sacha inside that long white box. Don't think. Don't. Hold it together. Look at Phil.

*Sacha wanted to share what he had, whether you were a friend or a stranger... I can't say travelling with him was always an easy road, but life for him wasn't an easy road... He did it honestly though... You just had to look in his eyes to see his heart... I think this is what I love about him most... That, and his cheeky smile when he'd been a bit naughty...*

I try to recall the order of ceremony I put together. Why didn't I bring it with me? Sally's on her feet again. Ah yes, she's about to read the final tribute from a friend of Sacha's who isn't here because he simply couldn't face it.

*For the time I knew him, he was good company, a great friend, full of jokes, and a very smart, strong guy who didn't fall for any bullshit. Although he was still young, for the time he was alive, he affected everybody he met...*

The curtains are closing around the coffin. I'm crash-landed back into reality. This is it. The committal. The incineration.

*Nam Myoho Renge Kyo. Nam Myoho Renge Kyo. Nam Myoho Renge Kyo. Nam Myoho Renge Kyo. Nam*

*Myoho Renge Kyo...*

Oh my God. I can't go there. I can't go there. Open the curtains again, please. Please. Oh my God. For Christ's sake, don't look at the curtains. Don't look at the curtains... Listen to the Incredible String Band singing the Celtic blessing you've chosen. Please, please turn the music up! Turn it up!

> *May the long time sun shine on you*
> *All love surround you*
> *And the pure light within you*
> *Guide you all the way home.*

Behind me, I can hear people weeping and blowing their noses. David puts his arm around me.

> *May the long time sun shine on you*
> *All love surround you*
> *And the pure light within you*
> *Guide you all the way home.*

I look up. People are drifting out of the crematorium. I watch my father, a few yards away, comforting my mother. She's in floods of tears again. I want to comfort her too, but then again, I just can't.

> *May the long time sun shine on you*
> *All love surround you*

*And the pure light within you*
*Guide you all the way home.*

We walk to the pub for the wake. Sally's telling me she felt Sacha behind her when she was speaking, giving her strength. I'm irritated that the shoes I bought with my mother two days ago from TK Maxx to match my outfit are half a size too big.

I arrive at the pub. A friend hugs me and enthuses that the atmosphere inside the crematorium was amazing, like floating on air. Another says she was surprised to feel joy amidst her grief. I sip wine and smile benignly, but don't touch the spread of food we've ordered. The Buddhist leader is finishing a cup of coffee and about to leave. I thank him. He tells me it's one of the most moving funerals he's ever conducted.

I want to glug back the wine but force myself to take it easy. Keep the show on the road. Friend after friend of Sacha's comes up to say hello or to introduce themselves. I'm taken by surprise; by no means are all of them crusties. I marvel at the beauty and sophistication of a couple of the young women, who are enthusing with emotion.

'He used to live with me in France.'

'We worked on X, Y or Z sound system together.'

'I hope he was wearing the locket I gave him when he died.'

'When we toured Eastern Europe, he was the only guy in the crew who never tried to hit on me. He respected women.'

Roberto is at the bar, getting very drunk. I look around.

Rebecca has disappeared. Where is she? Olga and her husband ask me to sit down and explain why this has happened. I take a deep breath and launch into Sacha's story, but my mind is still on Rebecca. She reappears at last and tells me she's been for a quiet wander around the crematorium gardens. Smoke? I want to ask her if she saw smoke coming out of the crematorium chimney. But I don't. I accept one of Phil's cigars instead. Smoke? I haven't smoked for a long time but it distracts me; I like it.

I place a couple of black plastic bin bags containing my son's possessions in a side room, and then alert his friends. An impromptu rugby scrum forms around the bags as they grab at precious keepsakes. The atmosphere is loaded with energy and emotion and for a brief few moments, I forget why I'm here. I look around. All of Sacha's friends and family are together for the first time in his life. Where is he?

Someone taps me on the shoulder; the mini-bus is waiting. We drag Roberto away from the bar. I say my farewells and walk out to the car park, relieved it's over. But a gnawing voice in my head tells me it isn't over. This is just the beginning. As the mini-bus pulls out into the road, I crane my neck in the direction of the crematorium, but it's too dark to see smoke…

I opened my eyes and shuddered. The sun was setting over Aguas Calientes. The bathers were drying themselves off and heading home. I felt cold, stiff and disorientated after yet another funeral reverie. Disassociation at Sacha's funeral had served as a valuable defence mechanism at the time; focusing on meaningless trivia helped me to survive the trauma and get through the day without breaking down entirely. After the event, though, certain scenes would replay themselves, over and over again, in my head. Seeing a black car in the road would trigger a memory of the black Mercedes hearse, and the image of the six serious young men carrying the white coffin into the crematorium would continue, for a few years, to haunt me day and night.

I collected Roberto, who was still sitting at the bar bantering away with a hippy-looking young Quechua waiter who teasingly called him 'Papa'. I envied the way Latin Americans could instantly become so chatty and familiar with each other, and regretted, not for the first time, my English reserve.

We stopped off at a family restaurant above the town for what promised to be a pleasant meal of orange trout. But Roberto, by now drink-fuelled, became over-loud. I didn't want any alcohol; I needed to be fully alert in the morning. My legs began to itch; I realised I was getting badly bitten.

I took a closer look at the unusual tropical plants surrounding our outside table and saw, to my horror, that they were covered in the dreaded sandflies I'd managed to avoid thus far in my travels to far-flung places. I stood up and announced to Roberto that I needed to be alone for the remainder of the evening to prepare myself for the following day. Giving him a peck on the cheek, I reminded him to set his alarm and left him to it.

# scattering sacha

## soulmates never die

The first anniversary of a death is important in Buddhism, as are the seventh day and the seventh week. The last two had been duly honoured back in England and, before leaving for Machu Picchu in the morning, I intended to commemorate Sacha's first anniversary.

Once back in my room, I placed Sacha's funeral invitation, which David had lovingly designed, on the small round coffee table that stood in the corner. The invitation consisted of images from childhood to manhood, superimposed onto a black-and-white photograph of Sacha as a smiling adolescent. I then proceeded to construct a little makeshift altar, on which I placed a candle, indicating light, a glass and a pencil, to serve as a bell, and some evergreen leaves, to symbolise the eternity of life. On a hostel ashtray which had 'Cusco' painted across it, I positioned three sticks of incense, representing the past, the present and the future. At the top of the table, I placed the small, portable Buddhist scroll I'd brought with me from England.

I opened my suitcase and took out the ashes. As I placed them underneath the table I recalled the moment when Sacha was conceived. Aged only nineteen, I knew something special had happened during that particular lovemaking session. I couldn't put it into words then and couldn't now. Are our lives pre-determined, I wondered? Was all of this?

'The distinction between past, present and future is no more than illusion,' Einstein insisted, 'even if a stubborn one.'

A Buddhist scholar once claimed that children were born into this world to enable their parents and others around them to attain Buddhahood. It was unlikely, I reflected, that I'd have continued practising had it not been for Sacha's difficulties over the years.

Along with certain other belief systems, Buddhism also says that we selected our parents, and chose to be reborn where we'd learn a new spiritual lesson. Had Sacha chosen us as parents? Was he trying to teach us something through his death? I thought about Roberto, and how we'd opened up to each other in the past week; how our mutual rancour had dissipated – it *had* to for Sacha's sake. Sometimes, we simply don't know the answers. But we do feel, and what I felt in my gut was that he wanted his father and me to heal thirty-odd years of resentment and grudges.

Satisfied with my altar, I laid out my clothes for the morning and climbed into bed for an early night. Once again, I sensed Sacha around me.

The dead speak to the living, but the living also speak to the dead:

My last night with your ashes, my beloved son. Part of me still can't believe this is actually happening...

The alarm on my mobile bleeps at 4.40am. It's the first anniversary of your death, my darling, but I'm already awake. I shower in a hurry, pull on a pair of navy cotton trousers, a light orange top and my favourite jewellery. I creep down the mosaic steps of the hostel to Roberto's room, to check he's awake. It's still dark but the room is empty. Your father's an insomniac. Smoke from his menthol cigarette drifts up from the garden. I return to my room, light the candle on the makeshift Buddhist altar and chant for an hour.

I put on my walking boots and your orange and black waterproof jacket, pick up the heavy black leather rucksack and go down for breakfast. To make conversation, I try to elicit sympathy for my bites, which are itching like mad, from a saturnine Roberto, telling him that sandflies carry something called leishmaniasis – deadlier than malaria – but he isn't interested. I try to hurry him with his coffee. We have to be on that 6.30am coach. He snaps at me, but we both know that today a row is out of the question.

The empty bus winds its way around the narrow mountain passes into sullen clouds. Roberto stares anxiously down into the cavernous drops. Heights don't bother me, but tourists do. We have to be there before they start pouring off their coaches.

It's what you don't see in all those Latin American travel brochures that makes Machu Picchu so awe-inspiring: the spectacular distant views of the snow-capped glacier summits of the Cordillera Vilcabamba, and down below, the deep, green valleys of the winding Río Urubamba. Machu Picchu's sublime scale, and astronomical geography, gives a sense of being perched on top of the world, within spitting distance of the stars.

The architect in Roberto is struck by the grandeur and mystery of the Inca temples and terraces. He finds the place utterly intoxicating, and feels the same sense of astonishment that I felt on my recce two days ago. But we don't have time to linger. As we hurry past the Intihuatana ('the hitching post of the sun'), which is an impressive astronomical pillar carved from stone and used by Inca priests to hitch the sun at the two equinoxes, I recollect, in a flash, our unplanned solstice reunion at Stonehenge. We quickly head onwards, past the Sacred Rock, towards the foot of the Huayna Picchu peak.

The Incas believed the mountain gods controlled weather and gave life or withheld it. Peaks became the places for sacred rites. We've come here for our own. You loved climbing mountains, my son. I knew as soon as you'd died, that this was where you wanted to be. After walking the Inca Trail, you'd arrived here at dawn to see the sun rise over a deserted Machu Picchu. Now you're sharing it with us. The place inspires spiritual feelings in Roberto, too. He knew he had to come here; that something between us had to heal.

Occasionally, the Incas would give offerings to the mountain gods in the form of human sacrifices. Children were considered purer than adults. The sacrificed child became a representative of the people, living with the gods forever after. Sacrifice was considered such an honour that the children were virtually deified. They died while unconscious or semiconscious, stupefied by a combination of *chicha* (corn beer) and altitude. Coca leaves, sacred to the Incas, were placed under their noses. I'm conscious of the parallels. You were no god, and at thirty you were no child, but you were certainly pure. Lyrics to Placebo's 'Pure Morning' swirl around my head. Their latest tour was called Soulmates Never Die.

We arrive at the bamboo gateway to Huayna Picchu. The peak is shrouded in mist. The gateway is open and the booth is empty. The Health and Safety Guardian hasn't clocked in yet. Good. All is going according to plan. We head for the plateau you led me to, on my recce. Roberto is behind me, struggling to keep up. His bronchitis has worsened and he has a pain in his leg. This altitude is nobody's friend.

Birdsong. The vegetation is lush and damp. I help Roberto clamber up and over the more challenging boulders. It feels heavy, so heavy carrying you in the rucksack on my back, as I'd once carried you in my belly.

We arrive at the plateau, near the base of the two peaks. I show your father the deep, deep drop down into the valley, miles below. You'll be safe from the feet of tourists here. We're in the clouds. The beauty of the spot pulsates. I take out the tiny Buddhist scroll. It's only about an inch square yet the calligraphy depicts the Mystic Law of Life and Death, the universe itself, and its interconnectedness with all phenomena. Eternity.

I place it on the edge of the flat shiny stone that forms the plateau. I take your ashes out of the orange silk pouch that Rebecca, the love of your life, has sewn and embroidered by hand, placing inside it a lock of her lovely black hair. Why is there so much orange around today, Sacha? It wasn't planned, at least not consciously.

I chant quietly as we take it in turns to grasp handfuls of your ashes. Your father and I scatter you north, south, east and west. To the valley and the river, the peaks close by and the glacier in the distance, the Temple of the Sun and the constellation of the Pleiades which rises from the peak of Huayna Picchu. I say a prayer to the *Apu* – the god of the mountain – as the Inca witch in Huasao instructed. Through tears I whisper, 'I'll meet you again, Sacha. I'll meet you again.'

Some of your wayward ashes still coat our trousers and shoes as we leave the plateau and scramble back down the boulders to the bamboo gate. A young Japanese man is about to make his ascent. On the other side of the bamboo gate, I take a photograph of the peak, now almost covered in mist. The Cordillera Vilcabamba is no longer visible, neither is the valley below.

We walk back through the ruins of the citadel, the cloud descending rapidly. I've never known Roberto go so long without a cigarette, but then I remember that smoking here

245

is forbidden. He hurries towards the entrance. I linger. Not wanting to leave this sacred sanctuary which is now your resting place, I rush up ancient steps to view the Temple of the Condor, but it's scarcely visible as the citadel becomes engulfed in heavy cloud. The peaks and terraces are totally invisible. I make my way back with difficulty, because now I can only see a few feet ahead.

Finally, at the exit, I look back and can see nothing. Nothing. The curtains have closed on this final leave-taking, as they did at your committal.

For someone who experienced abuse and torment, yet cherished the unfathomable and the mystic, I cannot imagine a more perfect place to be. A place that Che Guevara claimed 'drives any dreamer to ecstasy'.

I make my way towards Roberto, who is hovering undercover at the cafeteria entrance, smoking hungrily. The rain is lashing down and we're completely engulfed in fog. In silence, we watch miserable, anoraked tourists flop off the coaches, complaining bitterly that they've come half way around the world to admire this famous site and they can't see a damn thing.

From the coach, I send a general text: *Sacha's ashes scattered at Machu Picchu Citadel 7.20am Peruvian time. Very sad but also very beautiful.*

The responses are swift: Rebecca, Emma and other friends of yours are in the woods in England. It's cold. They've lit a fire and are playing your favourite music and sharing happy memories. David says he felt my pain during the scattering, then our living room filled with sunlight and the rose fragrance from the incense burner you gave him for Christmas flooded the room.

Suzanne, your aunt, has held a special ceremony in the west of Ireland. From Lagos, our dear friend Dr Afolabi responds: 'The mountains are the home of the gods. Sacha is our senior now.' And from Jake in Los Angeles: 'Hey – it's nearly 3am. The sun is rising over Peru. For no reason wind chimes are clanging in a dark steady rain. Goodbye Sacha – I love you.'

Back at Gringo Bill's, Margarita scans our faces with warm concern. She smiles tearfully and tells us that she's decided to take the urn from the mantelpiece and scatter the ashes of her son William at Machu Picchu.

In the bleak, wet afternoon, your father and I sit in semi-sacred silence in a restaurant beside the wild, roaring Agua Caliente River. I find the river soothing. Roberto says it makes him feel mad. Pisco Sours. Untouched food. Cigarettes. Coffee and flaming sambuca: Roberto's idea but not a good one. I burn my hair. Roberto puts his hand on the rim of the glass. It's so hot that it burns a scar into the palm of his hand, the shape of a crescent moon.

# empty rucksack

## free at last

We returned to Cusco by train the following day and spent the night at Incas Dreams. Alfredo was anxious to know whether everything had gone according to plan at Machu Picchu. I reassured him that it had. The next morning we said a warm, sad farewell.

Roberto and I had to take separate flights back to Lima, where I'd pre-booked us into the Hotel San Antonio Abad in Miraflores. My flight was delayed by two hours and the free hotel airport pick-up wasn't there to meet me. I eventually arrived, hungry and irritated, to find Roberto, still ill with bronchitis, hungry and irritated too. Again, miraculously, we avoided a row.

We went out for *cerveza* and *ceviche* in a restaurant nearby, and then took a taxi to the bay that was famous for its spectacular sunsets; it didn't disappoint. Sitting together on the hotel terrace under the stars that evening, we agreed it had been a difficult but worthwhile trip for us both, and that Sacha had wanted to share with us the wonders of Machu Picchu. Roberto's flight to Bogotá was very early the following morning, so we said our goodbyes and went to bed.

At breakfast, the hotel receptionist handed me an envelope. Inside was an unexpected cheque and a note from Roberto, thanking me for my kindness in Peru, and for being so understanding. My God! That was a first. It struck me that this trip had been the only time in living memory that I hadn't been asking him for something in the way of help or money for Sacha. We had both arrived in Peru estranged from one another and had parted, after so many years, as close friends. In this unfamiliar land, my son's father and I had made peace at last.

Back in Atlanta again, mission accomplished. But I felt as flat and empty as my rucksack. At US passport control, I'd queued for over an hour only to be aggressively quizzed, yet again: 'Why did you go to Peru? Why are you travelling on your own?'

Uniformed US soldiers, mainly black and Hispanic, were traipsing lethargically around the airport, en route to Iraq and Afghanistan. Everyone, including myself, appeared to be moving in slow motion. I had hours to kill before my flight to London. Mooching about, I spotted a sign directing passengers to a Martin Luther King exhibition on one of the concourses. As I made my way towards it I remembered that Atlanta was King's birthplace. Two years earlier, I'd written the text for a touring exhibition that had included a section on King. The wording on the banner of the last panel of the Atlanta exhibition, which followed on from the panel depicting his assassination, was the same that I'd chosen: 'Free at last!'

As I walked away from the exhibition with King's voice resounding in my head – 'Free at last! Free at last! Thank God Almighty we are free at last!' – I couldn't help noticing that the toilet cleaners and serving staff in the airport were mainly black. In a gift shop, I overheard a couple of rednecks complaining about all the 'n----- trinkets' for sale in the airport. After all King's efforts, had nothing changed? I wondered. Would nothing change for me?

As two hours still remained before my flight was due to be called, I decided there was nothing left for it but to head for the grotty airport bar I'd endured last time around. I sat down at the sad Formica table and ordered another absurdly expensive glass of Pinot Grigio. My waitress bore a striking resemblance to Rosa Parks, the black woman from Atlanta who lit the fuse of the civil rights movement when she refused to give up her seat on a bus to a white person.

It was Friday evening and the airport was getting busier and busier. Suddenly, the bar was full. As I sipped my wine I watched Rosa Parks glide elegantly up and down the bar, performing a kind of ballet around the tables as she wiped them with unusual grace and expertise. My spirits were lifting. I ordered a second glass of Pinot Grigio. What the hell, I thought; I can sleep it off on the plane.

The amalgam of songs and music David had collated for my trip continued randomly playing on my iPod and they all seemed bizarrely appropriate to Sacha. Was it a coincidence, or had he planned it that way? U2's 'Two Hearts Beat As One' ignited a poignant memory.

I couldn't face attending Sacha's inquest. Some years earlier, a TV production company which was considering making a drama series about coroners had employed me, as a writer, to attend an inquest into the death of a schizophrenic young man. Squeamish by nature, I found the graphic details of the autopsy deeply disturbing and broke down in tears when discussing my findings with the producer and script editor. Inquests and autopsies – I just couldn't go there again; especially when the deceased in question was my own son.

David had attended inquests when he was in the police force, and kindly offered to go on my behalf. I spent the day working in London, trying desperately to block out what was taking place in a certain court in Brighton. When I returned home, David, who was working nights, had already left for work. On the kitchen table he'd deposited a plastic bag the police had handed him after the inquest. It contained the items that had been on Sacha's person when they'd taken his body away.

With trembling hands, I opened it. There was some cash, various bracelets and medallions, and the thick woven cord that he wore around his neck, even when he went to bed. Attached to the cord were his harmonica, the keys to his flat and my house, and a cigarette lighter with flashing lights that I'd recently bought for him in France. I held the cord to my face. I could smell my son.

'Sacha! Sacha!' I cried out, 'How am I ever going to live without you?'

'Two Hearts Beat As One' blasted through my head.

The unsurprising verdict, David informed me the next day, was death from a heroin overdose. The kindly coroner apparently made a point of saying that the psychiatrist from the most recent drugs programme had said in his report that he'd been 'very impressed' by Sacha, and that many healthcare and drugs practitioners had acknowledged the help and support I'd given him.

The bar was packed now. A middle-aged guy sat down opposite me, all trussed up in a silver suit and rodeo gear. Surreal. By now, I was listening to a Pink Floyd song from *The Division Bell* about Syd Barrett, the brilliant former member – the 'golden boy' who had 'lost the light in his eyes' on drugs. I started to tear up. The rodeo guy was staring at me. Suddenly I wanted desperately to be back home with David again. My flight was announced. I hurried to the departure gate, listening to 'Thank You For The Days' by the Kinks.

On the plane, a black guy with long dreads sitting in the

seat next to mine opened a copy of the *International Herald Tribune*. He turned the page and there was a big colour picture of Machu Picchu. Yes, I reflected, I'd found the citadel magnificent and much of what I'd seen in Peru awe-inspiring, but the country had also, at times, frustrated and scared me.Overall I had mixed feelings about Peru – and Peru, I felt, had mixed feelings about itself. The same could be said of Sacha. It's too easy to slip into idealising the dead. Like the living, their lives are a mixture of the exceptional, the banal, and a whole lot in between.

Górecki's third symphony came on my iPod again. Now I was ready to hear it. I closed my eyes and saw Sacha's handsome face. This sublime music was so my son: the jangled instruments, the taut, jagged yet structured harmonies, all flowing out of a crazy cacophony. The intricate, heart-rending crescendos following on the heels of scarcely audible lulls and calms; the pain; the anguish; the cravings; the depths; the longing; the redemption. Underpinning it all, a feeling of foreboding: an unnerving sense that something unforeseen and uncontrollable was about to burst out and shatter everything; a heralding of death. And beneath the lurking sorrow, an aching beauty languished: the mad, sad beauty of Sacha and his life.

The plane took off into the night sky. I felt satisfied that I'd accomplished what I'd set out to achieve. Now my son belonged to the universe.

He was Free at Last.

# back home

## grief: the early years

Once home, I spent the first few weeks in something of a daze, tending to my infected sandfly bites and processing my time in Peru. It hadn't been my intention to traipse around the country alone with Sacha's ashes, but the trip had certainly satiated my desire to respect my son's life right up until the very end.

Travel, I reflected, can prove transformative in ways which we least anticipate. 'Travel far enough, you meet yourself,' writes David Mitchell in *Cloud Atlas*, one of the books I read on my travels. The trip certainly strengthened my resilience in body and soul and helped cure my claustrophobia. It also healed my relationship with Roberto. In Peru I stumbled upon parts of myself hitherto unknown. And yes, I also discovered Pisco Sours.

Certain experiences in the country reconnected me with

the joy and adventure inherent in life and brought me closer to Sacha. For us both, Machu Picchu, the sacred citadel of the gracious Incas, with its spine-tingling vistas and celestial mysteries, represented a distillation of all that is good and beautiful on this planet; a welcome retreat from the painful worlds of abuse, addiction and loss.

Not long after my return I came across the story of a bereaved young mother called Kisagotami, who, 2,550 years ago, begged the Buddha to restore her dead child to life. The Buddha instructed her to first collect a mustard seed from every dwelling where no one had died. She duly trudged from door-to-door, but was unable to collect a single seed. Kisagotami came to the realisation that death was universal. She went ahead and buried her child. Encounters with warm-hearted Peruvians, like Alfredo who had lost his mother, and Margarita who had lost her son, helped me to reach the same conclusion as Kisagotami. I stopped asking, Why me? Instead I to began to ask, Why not me?

All well and good, I remember thinking, but where was I now on my grief journey? My son might be free at last, but what about me?

An acquaintance of ours who had been unable to attend Sacha's funeral emailed me the day after it with her apologies and asked whether I now had 'closure'. At the time the question struck me as so ridiculous that I actually laughed. When I returned from Peru I was asked that same question several times – always from someone who had never, like the woman who sent the email, been bereaved.

Did these folk seriously believe that the whole messy business of grief is done and dusted once you've scattered your beloved's ashes? They were, I came to realise, simply seeking reassurance, consciously or unconsciously, that getting over losing someone was more like recovering from a bad bout of flu. But, oh, wouldn't it be wonderful, I remember thinking, if that really were the case...

I don't think there can ever be closure when we've lost someone – unless we want to wipe clean the slate of their (and our) very existence. None of my friends or family members, I'm happy to say, ever tried to tell me it was time I 'moved on'. But, over the years, a number of my clients have complained that they've been subjected to this thoughtless piece of advice so often dished out to the bereaved. One client who had lost her partner of nine years six months earlier came to see me for counselling – not for her loss but because she felt close to committing matricide. Her mother, on a daily basis, would tell the grieving woman via text message, phone call or in person that she really needed to be moving on. The final straw came when she suggested my client should register with Tinder. The mother's anxiety at having to witness her daughter's distress was clearly the reason behind her insensitive insistence that she 'moved on', but my client rightly perceived her mother's attitude as bullying; devoid of respect for her grieving process. Grief, and the processing of it, is a very personal journey.

I found the second year of loss more difficult than the first. This, I came to discover, is the case for many who have lost a loved one. Shock has a numbing affect in that first year. In addition to winding up their estate, there are also so many busying practical tasks related to the deceased to deal with which help maintain a connection of sorts. In my case this had included my preparations for visiting Peru. Come the second year, the grim reality that you will never see, touch, smell or speak to your beloved again really starts to sink in. For me, the pain of missing the physical presence of my son became quite visceral. While he remained in the forefront of *my* mind he no longer occupied that prime position for my nearest and dearest. Discussing Sacha with friends and family in the first year had helped to keep his memory alive, and I felt less alone in my grief. They might have 'moved on' by that second year, but I certainly hadn't.

Work, in those early years, was often a useful distraction from the pangs of loss and the unprocessed memories that would pop up uninvited. Sometimes I experienced an empathy bypass. A wealthy client sat opposite me one day, bawling her eyes out because her husband had forgotten to pre-book her a pedicure at the Reykjavík spa they had stayed at the previous weekend. It had ruined her break, she claimed. Her world and mine. Part of me felt like spewing out my own miseries by way of giving her a reality check, but I somehow managed to keep the empathy mask on.

Episodes such as this did, however, encourage me to challenge my judgementalism. Can we ever really know the extent of another's pain? As it transpired, the missing pedicure was, for this woman, just another example of her partner's waning affection, which would eventually lead to their separation.

More bereaved clients appeared in my consulting room than ever before in those first few years after losing Sacha. A Jungian psychologist would have called this synchronicity: the universe mirroring my newly acquired, bereaved status. I came to acknowledge that prior to my own loss my understanding of the many manifestations of grief had been fairly limited. I set myself the task of learning as much as I could about grief and mourning.For starters, I'd never really understood the difference between the two. Grief, I discovered, relates to the thoughts and feelings that accompany a loss – from sadness to anger to longing to be with the person who has passed. Mourning, on the other hand, is how those feelings of grief are manifested in public – such as wearing black, or daily visits to the beloved's grave.

I began to notice that for some people there exists a hierarchy of grief. This was brought home to me in a magazine interview with a well-known actor whose baby had recently died. He said he felt furious when anyone bemoaned the loss of a grandparent; his loss, he believed, was so much worse. But I came to appreciate that the loss of a grandparent can sometimes mean a great deal more than that of a parent, a sibling or even a partner. The degree of pain is relative – dependent on the nature and intensity of that lost relationship. A client of mine claimed he was more affected by the death of his dog than by that of his mother.

One of the cruellest griefs I encountered while exploring loss in its manifold manifestations was 'complicated grief'. A distressed young woman whose best friend had recently been killed in a motorbike accident came to me for bereavement counselling. She struck me as being, by nature, quite insecure. Convinced that this friend of hers since childhood fancied her new boyfriend, my client had stopped speaking to her the month before the accident. She was distraught to later learn that her deceased friend had actually disliked this new boyfriend of hers and was devastated to have been ghosted. Needless to say, the young woman was struggling with self-recrimination and guilt. She couldn't forgive herself.

Complicated grief such as this is torturous. After witnessing a number of similar scenarios, I've made sure that I don't get sucked into Mexican standoffs, and I do everything possible to smooth out any disagreements with friends and family. I encourage my clients to do the same. Death can strike at any time. To this day I feel so relieved that Sacha and I were on good, loving terms when he passed away.

I was fortunate, too, never to get stuck in a grief-related depression like the late Queen Victoria – who would have been awarded the equivalent of an Oscar for mourning if such a thing existed. She described in a letter how 'those paroxysms of despair and yearning and longing and of daily, nightly longing to die…for the first three years never left me'. Even once those three years were up, Victoria wore black for the next forty. Servants were instructed to continue laying out Albert's pyjamas at night and to take his shaving gear and hot water to his room every morning. There was, of course, a strong element of denial in all of this: a refusal to accept that Albert was encased in a tomb in St George's Chapel, Windsor, and not about to come striding through the palace gates.

Stuck grief and prolonged mourning like Victoria's – sometimes known as 'persistent, complex or chronic bereavement disorder' – has, I've noticed, a tendency to set in when the bereaved has been highly dependent on the one who has passed. Since she married at a young age, Victoria's ability to think for herself and trust her own judgement was negligible. She relied on Albert to make decisions for her – from affairs of state to which bonnet she should wear.

A client of mine in his sixties, whose 'other half', as he referred to his late partner, had, during their long relationship, dealt with all the couple's household bills, DIY, car and computer problems and other tedious stuff, while he had focused on the kitchen and the garden, found himself at a loss when it came to coping with day-to-day life on his own. He reported feeling 'inadequate, useless, a waste of space – half a person'. To avoid additional suffering when a loved one dies, it's a good idea, in any relationship, to work at forging an independent, capable, resilient self. Unsurprisingly, this grieving gentleman, who found daily life such a challenge after his partner died, succumbed to clinical depression.

As I began seeing more clients who presented with bereavement issues, I noticed that quite a few would describe themselves as depressed, when in fact they were simply grieving. The difference, I realised, isn't always that clear. Grief and depression share similar symptoms:

anxiety; lethargy; a bleak outlook; frequent tears. But it's still possible to feel emotions such as peace and joy while grieving – especially when out in nature, on a relaxing holiday – or even after a good, therapeutic cry. With a full-on clinical depression, upbeat emotions quite simply don't get a look-in – even if you've just won the lottery.

For someone who is so depressed that they can't crawl out from under the duvet in the morning – or who needs a few shots of vodka to do so – an anti-depressant, known as an SSRI (selective serotonin reuptake inhibitor), can help. When grief is prolonged or complicated, levels of the neurotransmitter serotonin, which promotes good mood, happiness and optimism, diminish. SSRIs block the reabsorption of serotonin into the body and in so doing can improve mood. So, for that matter, can having the support, the courage and the self-love to work at building a new life.

In the early years of their bereavement, many people are prescribed anti-depressants by their GPs. I never felt the need to take them myself. Not that I have anything against them. Whenever grief started to get the better of me, I was fortunate to have my Buddhist practice to fall back on. Even if it felt like an effort sometimes, I simply upped my chanting.

'Comforters' that friends and clients claim have helped them to get through the first few tough years of grief include: getting a dog; taking ayahuasca; self-harming; moving home; alcohol; rock climbing; Botox; visiting a spiritual retreat. Unfortunately, certain 'comforters' that help to numb the pain can too often become unwanted addictions.

For me, creativity – in my case writing – provided a welcome release from pain. Music, too, proved wonderfully cathartic. I especially liked listening to the Icelandic band Sigur Rós when I was in a grief funk. The singer Jónsi Birgisson's strange vocalisations, known as *Vonlenska* – an imaginary, made-up language of his own – somehow resonated with my raw, roller-coaster emotions.

What really lightened my sorrow in those early years was coming across a relatively new approach to grief known as 'continuing bonds'. Modern grief experts are now pretty much in agreement that successful grieving doesn't involve the breaking of the emotional bond with the deceased, rather its perpetuation. Other cultures have for centuries embraced this way of thinking but it's still relatively new in the West, where, by and large, grief is viewed along the lines of a painful affliction from which you will recover in time.

'Continuing the bond' with your deceased loved one involves continuing to communicate with them. For some this can mean establishing a special grief space, with, for example, a candle, photos or any object belonging to the loved one that has a meaningful association. I found – and continue to find – this a moving and also an energising way to maintain a spiritual connection with my son.

Forging an enduring bond can be comforting and even wondrous. Sometimes that bond can be movingly reinforced: After hearing through the grapevine of his death, Sacha's former Australian girlfriend, Angie, sent me some photographs she'd taken of him in South America.

They gave me a huge lift. Sacha told me once that he only felt truly alive when exploring other countries, their landscapes, culture and customs. In these photographs he's in his element: rock-climbing, fishing, swimming, hugging a statue of Simon Bolivar, the liberator of South America, at the summit of a mountain he'd just scaled. They served as a precious reminder that, in his short and often anguished life, my son experienced the excitement of travel, and also knew happiness and love.

David and I commissioned a sculpture from Phil, Sacha's best friend, called *El Viajero* (The Traveller). The abstract sculpture reflects Sacha's psyche: in disarray below, *El Viajero*'s welded steel shards then reach out to lands beyond and stars above, to freedom.

I had Angie's photos blown up and they formed the backdrop to the unveiling of *El Viajero*. It was a joyful occasion. Sacha's family were all present, along with those friends who shared his love of being on the road. Emma was expecting her first child. Rebecca brought along a mutual friend of hers and Sacha's, whom she has since married. Witnessing Sacha's struggles with dyslexia over the years inspired Rebecca to seek out work with a dyslexia foundation, and later with a special needs educational publisher.

Sacha would certainly have approved of how Rebecca and his friends have moved on.

When the giant wave hit South East Asia on Boxing Day 2004, Sacha was spending Christmas with me. He died a week later. Four years on, I found myself at Khao Lak in

Thailand, the Thai resort that had been worst hit by the tsunami. Even the Thais' beloved king had lost a grandson there. Strangely enough, it was a very healing experience. I met people who had lost everything, including family members. They'd just had to roll their sleeves up and rebuild their homes and their lives. I felt less alone with my own loss.

On the afternoon of the fourth anniversary of Sacha's death, I went for a lengthy walk along Khao Lak beach, arriving at a stretch of sand that was virtually deserted. To my amazement, I saw a decrepit, rusty lifeguard tower, identical to the one I'd scrambled up in the nightmare I'd had of being engulfed by a huge black wave in the run-up to Sacha's death. And as I gazed up at the rusty tower, I acknowledged, for the first time, that I had managed to survive my personal tsunami.

# as time goes by

## challenge and transformation

Grief shape-shifts over time and for me, at least, the pain intensity of those earlier years has certainly lessened. It's now almost twenty years since I lost Sacha. I've accepted that there will always be an ache, a yearning, a 'where are you now?' question in my head. But I'm also one of the lucky ones. I've somehow managed to keep my head above the grimy waters of survivor's guilt.

I've experienced additional losses during these two decades – one of the first being Sacha's father, Roberto, who sadly died a couple of years after our return from Peru. Two very close friends also passed away in quick succession, and, more recently, I've lost my father and my mother. While each of these deaths has hit me pretty hard, if I'm honest, not one of them came anywhere near the life-imploding impact of Sacha's. I don't believe you ever get over the loss of a loved one, but you do learn to live with it. As time has passed, I've encountered a different set of challenges. I've also experienced unforeseen gains.

One of the harder aspects of loss is that we find ourselves having to inhabit a different reality and a new personal – and often social – identity. I sometimes find it difficult meeting new people. Topics of discussion invariably gravitate from where you live, to what you do and then to how many children or grandchildren you have. Depending on who has asked the question I might answer it – or I might try to change the subject. I feel I'm somehow betraying Sacha and my own experience of motherhood if I say I haven't any children. But being honest can often mean I have to put up with people's awkwardness and that ghastly, glib phrase, 'I'm sorry for your loss'.

I've learned that we can distract our conscious mind from the sometimes inconvenient rumblings of grief – or block them out with displacement activities such as mindless scrolling or compulsive biscuit eating – but we can't control our unconscious mind. This is where I've found grief has become most vibrant and active. Time doesn't exist in this pesky, unfathomable unconscious of ours, nor is it able to distinguish between a wish and a reality. My dreams, these days, are often vivid: they feature Sacha as a child or a teenager and occasionally as an adult. The years between his passing and the present time dissolve. Sometimes we're having fun together, at other times I'm searching for him in vain, or discovering, yet again, that he's no longer alive. A heavy loss dream, even after all this time, can affect my mood for the entire day and sometimes beyond, whereas a happy dream is both uplifting and reassuring.

A common later-stage grief conundrum is how many photographs and artefacts that belonged to the beloved do you continue to keep on display once the wall-plastering phase of early grieving has passed. It's usually a very personal matter – unless it impacts on the life of another. A client of mine complained that his wife still had a bust, a portrait and a large number of framed photographs of her late, revered father scattered around the house fourteen years after his passing. He hadn't cared much for his father-in-law when he was alive – and even less so now. His wife continued to sing her father's praises at every available opportunity. She unfavourably compared her husband to this pedestalised parent, who, in death, had morphed into a demigod for one half of the couple and a malign presence for the other.

I'm wary of the home-as-permanent-shrine set-up, because it encourages a backward-looking mindset. For me less is more. While there were plenty of photographs of Sacha on display in the early years, now they're kept, along with other precious items, in a lovely white glass cabinet which sits below the portrait I commissioned my sister Sally to paint, based on one of my favourite photos of him. A thriving sweetheart vine that Sacha once bought me sits on top of the cabinet. When the mood takes me I open the cabinet and have a chat with him.

Anniversaries, and the heavy moods and memories that often accompany them, still remain hugely significant over time – even when they haven't been consciously remembered. In her book *Grief and Grieving*, Elisabeth Kübler-Ross describes how bereaved children in the care system will manifest difficult behaviour on the anniversary of their parents' deaths – even, extraordinarily, children too young to understand the calendar. The conscious mind may have forgotten, but the unconscious certainly hasn't.

I've discovered that anniversaries can also be joyful and provide an opportunity to reaffirm the bond. I usually celebrate Sacha's late-August birthday with a bottle of something bubbly, somewhere warm, in beautiful surroundings. As I dust off happy memories, I feel him around me, willing me on to embrace life – to 'live life' for him.

For many of us who have been bereaved, proximity to death, and the pain of loss, give rise, over time, to existential questions – not simply about what may or may not happen in the hereafter, but concerning the meaning of life. Is life, in the words of the 17th-century philosopher Thomas Hobbes, 'nasty, brutish, and short'? Or does a brutal wake-up call to life's transitory nature imbue it with a piquant vitality?

Some people certainly develop a post-bereavement *carpe diem* mentality, determined to make the most of every moment to ensure they have no regrets when they die. I've seen behaviours that began as grief distractions or comforters transform into passions. One young woman who had lost her paragliding brother to cancer learnt to paraglide herself for the sole purpose of scattering his ashes.

This later became a much-loved hobby which she credited with helping her through her grief. This approach is so preferable to those 'ashes to ashes, dust to dust' depressed clients I've seen who have, in some cases, developed a terror of the nothingness they believe awaits them after death – which puts the kibosh on their ever finding enjoyment in daily life.

The loss of someone very close has, I've noticed, a tendency to open up new religious or spiritual paths – and also, sometimes, to abruptly shut them down. Those who abandon their faith are unable to believe that a benign deity could possibly permit the pain they're experiencing. Others embrace religion and spirituality for the first time, in search of meaning and in the hope they'll be reunited with their beloved in the afterlife. While my Buddhist practice has remained stable over the years, I've certainly become interested in accounts of near-death experiences (NDEs). This came about through reading a convincing account by the brilliant Swiss analytical psychologist Carl Jung of his own NDE.

Following a severe heart attack in 1944, Jung found himself up in space, looking down at the blue planet earth: 'I felt as though I were safe in the womb of the universe – in a tremendous void, but filled with the highest possible feeling of happiness. This is eternal bliss, I thought. This cannot be described; it is far too wonderful.'

Jung's doctor managed to resuscitate him, but instead of feeling grateful, Jung was furious at being returned to a 'boxed-in' three-dimensional existence and fell into a deep depression for several weeks. The experience had a profound affect on his later life and work.

The redoubtable Kübler-Ross and her team succeeded in collecting experiences from over 25,000 people from different cultural and religious backgrounds whose stereotypical NDEs included the post-death 'tunnel of light' (as portrayed in countless cheesy movies)and being greeted by deceased loved ones.

Another convincing advocate of NDEs is the neuropsychiatrist Dr Peter Fenwick, a Fellow of the Royal College of Psychiatrists and president of the British branch of the International Association for Near-Death Studies. Fenwick has managed to bring a scientific yet humane perspective to a phenomenon which is ultimately unprovable in this lifetime. For some, NDEs are simply a grief-balm fantasy; for others, myself included, the thought that we'll meet our loved ones again in some shape or form is undoubtedly comforting.

Deep suffering and loss can also lead to what is known as post-traumatic growth: we forge a deeper connection with, and understanding of life which, hitherto, we may have taken for granted. Much like travel, loss can enhance our knowledge and appreciation of what it means to be human. It can become a transformative entry into a new life – one of more compassionate engagement and value creation.

Although it was gruelling, my journey with Sacha certainly deepened my connectedness with, and compassion for, others. To help fill the emptiness left by my loss, I took on board the Buddhist concept of turning poison into medicine and attempted to create some value out of Sacha's suffering and my own. I set up my own counselling consultancy, Greenlight Healing. Many of the clients I continue to work with have suffered abuse, addiction or bereavement. I find it gratifying that I'm able to offer my abused and addicted clients the help I was unable to extend to my own son until it was too late. Sometimes I tell bereaved clients that I, too, have been closely bereaved. I don't divulge any details but I've found that this disclosure helps promote understanding on a deeper level and, in so doing, strengthens the therapeutic alliance. They know I know what deep grief feels like.

My involvement with various charities would never have come about had I not lost Sacha. I've contributed my experience to Anyone's Child, a charity which advocates safer drug control and calls for the legal control and regulation of the drug market. I was also invited by Elizabeth Burton-Phillips – the founder of the charity DrugFAM (now known as Addiction Family Support), which provides support to families and friends who have been bereaved by addiction, and who herself lost a son to heroin – to be a guest speaker at one of the charity's annual conferences. I posted my experience and later made a short film about the Forgiveness Project, founded in 2004 by my fellow Buddhist, Marina Cantacuzino, which uses the real stories of victims and perpetrators to explore concepts of forgiveness, reconciliation and conflict resolution.

A surprising yet gratifying example of how Sacha's death has inadvertently impacted the lives of others is the success of the award-winning animation *Confessions of an English Ant-Eater* written, illustrated and directed by my nephew Alex Crumbie. A creative in the true sense of the word, Alex has published six illustrated chapbooks which have also been translated into Japanese. (A chapbook is a small booklet containing ballads, poems or tales.) Alongside writing for *Ethical Consumer* magazine, he is a member of the *avant garde* rock band Legs On Wheels.

Alex was cycling through France when *Junkie Buddha*, an earlier edition of this book, came out. He hadn't, at that time, read the book but was upset by articles he saw in the national press that mentioned Sacha's abuse and addiction – something that he hadn't fully grasped at the age of thirteen, when his cousin died. Alex had also recently read Thomas De Quincey's infamous *Confessions of an English Opium-Eater*. First published in 1821, the book is a colourful literary memoir which details the author's opium addiction.

Alex has said he loved and was inspired by much of the art and music that had resulted from drug-taking, but that the glamorisation of hard drug use made him very uncomfortable: 'Sacha's battle with heroin and subsequent death had shown me the very real consequences of drug addiction and was a stark contrast to the mystique associated with drug use, particularly with opium and heroin.'

Originally a poem, *Confessions of an English Ant-Eater* metamorphosed into an illustrated chapbook, and finally into a short animated film narrated in verse and accompanied by a moody, folk noir soundtrack. Funded by the BBC and the Arts Council, the animation premiered on BBC Four in December 2021. It tells the story of a rebellious boy called Thomas, who, despite his parents' admonitions, gradually becomes addicted to eating ants. The end result is that Thomas, in a desperate bid to get his fix, climbs into an ant nest, only to find himself devoured by the ants he sought to consume.

When I first read, in chapbook form, this humorous tale of an overdose, it gave me a jolt. I had to take a few deep breaths. But I knew my warm-hearted, sensitive nephew well enough to realise that the motive informing its creation was essentially an altruistic one. Alex had once worked for a charity that ran poetry workshops in schools. Presenting this painful subject in such an original and accessible form was a means through which he could counteract the lure of dangerous drugs – especially to a younger generation.

Alex was concerned about my possible reaction – that I might consider the story insulting. He said: 'It was never intended to be facetious... I believe that I was trying to process my cousin's death by turning it into something more manageable, while also providing a cautionary tale that would provide some balance to the glamour of opium found in De Quincy...' He was still worried, he told me, about my possible reaction years later when he made it into a film, and was very relieved that I liked it.

As well as being screened in the UK, *Confessions of an English Ant-Eater* has been selected for international film festivals in Germany, Brazil, Italy, Slovakia and Japan – where it won an award. 'It has been brilliant,' Alex told me recently, 'travelling around the world with my film and speaking about it at film festivals. This has given me the opportunity to talk about what inspired it and tell people a bit about your and Sacha's stories.' Only last month, Alex asked me for a photograph of Sacha and myself to include in a slide-show talk to accompany a screening of the film at the Portico Library in Manchester – a historic library that Thomas De Quincey visited.

'It's very hard,' Alex says, 'to understand the effects of our actions, but I hope this film has brought some positivity to the world, and given those who have viewed it enjoyment and something to ruminate on.'

It surely has. I applaud the hard-hitting yet entertaining film and hope it encourages all age groups to consider the dangers of addiction and think twice before taking a mindless nosedive into hard drugs.

One of my reasons for wanting to write this book was to demonstrate, with my own life, that it's possible to survive every parent's worst nightmare – the death of a daughter or son. Writing and travel continue to afford me much pleasure, likewise my work as a therapist. And after all we've been through as a couple, David and I remain close and happy.

I miss my son's physical presence, but I continue to have a strong sense of connection with him – albeit spiritual. I talk to him still, and 'hear' him talk to me. Like Sacha, I still enjoy a good moan from time to time, but, overall, I treasure my life.

It *is* possible to have a life after death – even a more meaningful one.

# acknowledgements

Research, such as that undertaken by Dr Lonny Shavelson in America, has been a source of inspiration in the writing of this book. His study of two hundred addicts, *Hooked* (2001), found that an alarmingly high proportion of his subjects had been sexually abused as children. These findings were corroborated in an article in the *Journal of the American Medical Association* which stated that the addiction rate for male, sexually abused children was 25 to 50 times higher than that for the rest of the population.

In a similar vein, *Tears on my Pillow, Voices in my Head*, the groundbreaking work presented by New Zealand clinical psychologist Dr John Read and University of Manchester researcher Paul Hammersley at the Institute of Psychiatry in London in 2006, convincingly argued that two-thirds of people diagnosed as schizophrenic have suffered physical or sexual abuse.

The work of several charitable organisations also helped inform the contents this book. Many adults who have been sexually abused in childhood carry into adulthood the toxic, guilty feelings of their abuser, and so are too ashamed to speak out. The National Association for People Abused in Childhood (NAPAC) has given many thousands of adults the courage to speak about their experiences and to begin a journey of recovery.

Families of addicts need support too, and this is something to which Elizabeth Burton-Philips, the author of *Mum, Can You Lend Me Twenty Quid?*, has dedicated her life since losing her son Nicholas, a heroin addict. To honour his memory, Elizabeth founded DrugFAM (recently renamed Addiction Family Support), a charity which supports families of the addicted and those who have been bereaved by addiction.

The Forgiveness Project, a charity founded by the journalist Marina Cantacuzino, has been instrumental in helping people around the world to move on from trauma and to forgive.

Members of the Buddhist organisation SGI-UK have provided ongoing compassion and support. The late Daisaku Ikeda, the Japanese president of SGI at the time of Sacha's death, who had also lost an adult son, sent me a personal message after my bereavement.

I would like to thank my agent, Jennifer Barclay, for suggesting this new edition. For the last ten years she has been an inspiring and invaluable support in all my literary endeavours. I'm very grateful to Dan Hiscocks at Eye Books for agreeing to publish this latest edition of my work and for continuing to publish such a bold and eclectic range of books. I would also like to thank Simon Edge who has proved to be an excellent and thorough editor. His editorial suggestions have certainly resulted in a tighter, more cohesive narrative. My thanks also go to Nell Wood who has produced a strikingly beautiful and original book cover, and to Clio Mitchell for her first-class typesetting. And finally, I remain profoundly grateful to David for his ongoing patience and love.

# related links

**Addaction**
UK drug and alcohol charity.
www.addaction.org.uk

**Alex Crumbie**
www.alexcrumbie.com
*Confessions of an English Ant-Eater* animation:
https://www.bbc.co.uk/programmes/p0b5p33q

**BACP – British Association for Counselling and Psychotherapy**
Government-accredited psychological therapists' register.
www.bacp.co.uk

**Care For The Family**
Bereaved parents' support.
www.careforthefamily.org.uk
029 2081 0800

## Childline
Support for young people under 19 years of age.
www.childline.org.uk
0800 1111

## The Compassionate Friends
Supporting bereaved parents and their families.
https://www.tcf.org.uk/
0345 123 2304

## Addiction Family Support (formerly DrugFAM)
Support for families bereaved by or having to cope with
addiction.
http://www.drugfam.co.uk
01494 442 777 (Office)
0300 888 3853 (Helpline)

## The Forgiveness Project
Encourages people to consider alternatives to resentment,
retaliation and revenge in relation to traumas.
www.theforgivenessproject.com

## Futuros Valores
Charitable refuge for street children in Barranquilla, Colombia.
www.divvol.org/futval

## Hearing Voices Network
For people who hear voices, see visions or have other unusual
perceptions.
www.hearing-voices.org

## Mind
Mental health charity.
www.mind.org.uk
0300 123 3393

**MOSAC – Mothers of Sexually Abused Children**
Support for non-abusing parents of abused children.
www.mosac.org.uk
0800 980 1958

**NAPAC – National Association for People Abused in Childhood**
Support and signposting for adult survivors.
www.napac.org.uk
0808 801 0331

**NSPCC – National Society for the Prevention of Cruelty to Children**
Report any concerns about a child.
www.nspcc.org.uk
0808 800 5000

**PDSA – People's Dispensary for Sick Animals**
Provides free veterinary services for the pets of needy owners in the UK.
www.pdsa.org.uk
0800 731 2502

**Samaritans**
Listening support for anyone struggling to cope.
www.samaritans.org
116 123

**SGI – Soka Gakkai International**
Socially engaged, worldwide Buddhist movement.
www.sgi.org

**SGI-UK**
www.sgi-uk.org
01628 773163

**Survivors UK**
Support for male adult survivors of sexual abuse.
www.survivorsuk.org

**UKNA – Narcotics Anonymous in the UK**
A non-profit organisation for anyone with a drug problem.
www.ukna.org
0300 999 1212

**We Are With You**
Drug, alcohol and mental health charity.
www.wearewithyou.org.uk

Also by Diane Esguerra

# The Oshun Diaries
*Encounters with an African goddess*

High priestesses are few and far between, white ones in Africa even more so. When Diane hears of a mysterious Austrian woman worshipping the Ifa river goddess Oshun in Nigeria, her curiosity is aroused.

It is the start of an extraordinary friendship that sustains her through the death of her son and leads to a quest to take part in Oshun rituals. Prevented by Boko Haram from returning to Nigeria, she finds herself at Ifa shrines in Florida amid vultures, snakes, goats' heads, machetes, a hurricane and a cigar-smoking god. Her quest steps up a gear when Beyoncé channels Oshun at the Grammys and the goddess goes global.

Mystifying, harrowing and funny, *The Oshun Diaries* explores the lure of Africa, the life of a remarkable woman and the appeal of the goddess as a symbol of female empowerment.

*An absolute joy to read... leads you on a spiritual journey where you feel as if you've been transported to Africa*
**Wrong Side of Forty**

*It was refreshing to read about a belief system that was so firmly rooted in the female form. This empowering and enlightening book reaffirmed my belief that you have to push out of your comfort zone at times, because you never, ever stop learning*
**Book Bound**

*A stunning, beautiful and complex memoir. Profoundly moving and enlightening*
**Cal Turner**

If you have enjoyed *Night Into Light*, do please help us spread the word – by putting a review online; by posting something on social media; or in the old-fashioned way by simply telling your friends or family about it.

Book publishing is a very competitive business these days, in a saturated market, and small independent publishers such as ourselves are often crowded out by the big houses. Support from readers like you can make all the difference to a book's success.

Many thanks.

Dan Hiscocks
Publisher, Eye Books